Living a
Safe Universe

A Book for Seth Readers

"Lynda Dahl takes the reader deep into the heart of Seth's teachings, and one emerges with a new vision and understanding of concepts that will transform one's personal world, and thus the world in general. Highly recommended for all Seth readers who wish to take Seth's material to a whole new level."
— **Rich Kendall, author of *The Road to Elmira* and member of Jane Roberts' ESP Class**

"I can only recommend this book to every Seth reader around the world. *Living a Safe Universe* inspires us to examine substantial ideas in the Seth material that lead us to a deeper understanding of ourselves in a larger context. A new kind of fascinating journey through the material."
— **Masa Nishio, founder of Seth Network Japan**

"I have no doubt that somewhere, some-when, in a cozy country den, Seth is lighting a cigar and raising a glass of brandy in celebration of *Living a Safe Universe*. This outstanding book is more than a 'must read' for anyone truly dedicated to understanding and living the Seth material – this book is essential!"
— **Lucy Gillis, author of *Dream Secrets: Unlocking the Mystery of Your Dreams*, and co-editor of the online magazine *Lucid Dreaming Experience***

"Lynda Dahl has studied the Jane/Rob/Seth material extensively and once again shares her understanding and insights. Practical methods are included to assist others in their journey into the self. Lynda's dedication to comprehending and applying the ideas is an inspiration to all of us."
— **Mary Dillman, ad hoc pro bono researcher and organizer of the Seth/Jane Roberts/Robert Butts material**

"I love this book. *Living a Safe Universe* brings us to a new understanding of the Seth material, and how to apply this understanding to trust. Lynda drives home the point that we are primarily consciousness which exists in the spacious present, as opposed to being an ego in time, and then explains why that fact changes the playing field entirely."
— Lawrence Davidson, member of Jane Roberts' ESP class and founder of the California Seth Conference

"As a 30+ year student of the Seth material, I looked forward to reading Lynda Dahl's new book. Not more five pages into it, all I found myself saying was...Wow! Lynda is able to draw on the Seth teachings and guide us through the 'why and how' it all works. And there is excitement and energy in the text. I highly recommend this book to all Seth readers."
— Jeff Kiefer, Clinical Case Manager and publisher of the website Seth Forums

"Coming at the Seth material from a new angle, Lynda Dahl takes us on a journey from a macro-view of the universe to how we can learn to trust ourselves in our lives and our creativity. Each chapter contains nuggets that explode on the printed page, that can be read and reread to gain more insight. Highly recommended."
— Richard Wolinsky, member of Jane Roberts' ESP class and syndicated talk show host

Some who have endorsed other books by Lynda Madden Dahl:

Robert F. Butts, co-creator of the Seth/Jane Roberts Books

Louise Hay, author of *You Can Heal Your Life* and *Empowering Women*

Fred Alan Wolf, Ph.D., author of *Mind into Matter* and *The Spiritual Universe*

Bruce Lipton, Ph.D., former Stanford University scientist and author of *The Biology of Belief, Spontaneous Evolution,* and *The Wisdom of Your Cells*

Norman Friedman, author of *Bridging Science and Spirit* and *The Hidden Domain*

Bernie Siegel, M.D., author of *Love, Medicine and Miracles*

Gerald G. Jampolsky, M.D., author of *Love is Letting Go of Fear*

Anne Meara, actor, playwright, and partner of Stiller and Meara comedy team

Willis Harman, Ph.D., past President, Institute of Noetic Sciences; author of *Global Mind Change*

Walter Eckhart, Ph.D, Professor, The Salk Institute

Richard Schneider, Ph.D., Chancellor, University of Global Education; co-founder, Radio for Peace Intl.

FINE PRODUCTS FROM THE WOODBRIDGE GROUP

by LYNDA MADDEN DAHL

Beyond the Winning Streak*
Using Conscious Creation to
Consistently Win at Life

Ten Thousand Whispers*
A Guide to Conscious Creation

The Wizards of Consciousness*
Making the Imponderable Practical

The Book of Fallacies
A Little Primer of New Thought
(with Cathleen Kaelyn)

Living a Safe Universe*
A Book for Seth Readers

* Paperback and eBook

by NORMAN FRIEDMAN

Bridging Science and Spirit
Common Elements in David Bohm's Physics,
The Perennial Philosophy and Seth

The Hidden Domain
Home of the Quantum Wave Function
Nature's Creative Source

Living a
Safe Universe

A Book for Seth Readers

Lynda Madden Dahl

Living a Safe Universe

Dahl, Lynda Madden, 1943—
Living a Safe Universe: A Book for Seth Readers / by
Lynda Madden Dahl

Library of Congress Control Number: 2012954741

Library of Congress Subject Headings:
New Age movement
Lightning Source (Firm)

Printed Book: ISBN 978-1-889964-13-3
eBook: ISBN 978-1-889964-14-0

This book is dedicated to readers of the Seth/Jane Roberts/Robert Butts material, those pioneering thinkers who eschew conventional ideas of reality and strike out on their own to uncover the truths behind creation. It is also dedicated, with boundless appreciation, to the brilliant triad themselves.

Jane Roberts - May 8, 1929-September 5, 1984
Robert F. Butts - June 20, 1919 - May 26, 2008

Contents

The inner natural leanings of all consciousness within the realms of your being now yearn for constructive change, clearer vision, to experience again their inherent sense of corporal spirituality, physical and psychic grace. They want to sense again the effortless motion that is their birthright.
—Seth, Dreams, "Evolution" and Value Fulfillment, Volume Two, *Session 941*

Introduction

I came out of San Francisco International Airport pulling my luggage and looking for the cab line. I was headed into San Mateo for a two-day workshop, which I had co-created and at which I was to be a presenter, for Seth Network International, a company I helped found. Off to my right, and nowhere near the cab line, was a man standing outside his vehicle, smiling as he caught my eye. He walked a couple paces toward me and asked if I needed a taxi. The problem was his vehicle had no cab markings, no roof sign. When I questioned him about it, he said his official taxi was in for repairs, and proceeded to hand me a business card embossed with his cab company's name.

I thought about it for a couple seconds and said okay. So, he placed my luggage in a messy trunk strewn with odds and ends, I climbed into the back seat, gave him my hotel's name and location, and off we went. Before we cleared the airport, I asked him how much he was going to charge me, seeing he had no meter. He thought a moment and said, "Forty dollars." I countered with twenty and he agreed.

As we came out of the airport, he seemed a little hesitant about which direction to take, but correctly swung south. That hesitation got my attention. I said, "You do know where my hotel is located, don't you?" He didn't earn my confidence when he hesitated yet again. I then rather logically queried, "Okay, how are you going to get directions without a dispatch radio?" He smiled brightly. So, I pulled out my cell phone, called the hotel's front desk, and asked directions. With a mental map now handy, I guided my cabbie to the hotel. We arrived, I paid him, we shared smiles, and that was that.

The name of the workshop I was presenting was titled "Living a Safe Universe: Trust and Its Pivotal Role in Conscious Creation." As I was preparing my final notes that evening, I thought about the cab driver and my ready acceptance of his good intent. And I thought how far I'd come in trusting I live safely in my reality. The road had been long and arduous, but I'd reached my goal and knew I'd never lose that acceptance of safety again. It is perhaps the greatest gift I've given myself, and I believe the raison d'être for my current existence, my ultimate lesson to be learned and explored this time around.

Seth and the Leap Beyond

I have lived with the Seth/Jane Roberts/Robert Butts material at the heart of my life since 1984. It has been a touchstone of such significance I blanch at the thought of life without it. The path not traveled leaves me giddy with relief, like a bullet missed, a tumble into flatness sidestepped. I cannot say it has been a path of assured happiness and success. I *can* say it has been a path laden with the *possibility* of happiness and success. And that alone is why I missed the bullet and the flatness that engulf so many. I had an out, if I chose to use it, one that brought not blind hope, but hope anchored in knowledge, and even in logic; and, eventually, trust.

In 1993, when I coined the phrase "conscious creation" while writing my first book, *Beyond the Winning Streak: Using Conscious Creation to Consistently Win at Life*, little did I know my life would become one ongoing experimental lab for the subject. And little did I know how little I knew. Not in its overall theory and concepts per se; and not in applications meant to help us feel the concepts intuitively, such as meditations and psychological time-outs, or psy-times. Nor in other applications, such as belief work, which help us to understand the immense implications of our thinking and emotions.

No, in 1993, I thought I had identified the facets of what I termed conscious creation, and would proceed through life safely, with little left to do other than to keep exploring Seth, work with my beliefs, continue to attempt to sense more of nonphysical reality, regularly talk to my inner self, and set goals. What more could possibly be needed in order to live with effortlessness and safety in my reality?

Excuse me while I wipe tears of laughter from my eyes.

When my world finally crumbled and fell around me, when the

pain was deep and enduring, when I couldn't seem to find my way out, when I wondered if it was even worth it to try, it confirmed a concern I'd had for years, a concern that I'd missed something of great significance in the Seth material, even though, at that point, I had no idea what it might be. I just knew I needed to find it or die trying. And that's how this book came into being.

The Gulf of Trust

Where were you in the 1990s? Where were you in your thinking, your beliefs, your attitudes, your fears, your trust? Who can remember such things, right? Most people don't give them serious thought at the time, let alone reminisce about them years later.

But, with every event you recall, every memory, you can tell precisely where you were in your beliefs, attitudes, fears and trust. Because, as Seth readers, we know it is not possible to encounter an event or memory that doesn't intimately reflect these issues, not necessarily within the outward event per se, but in what got us there in the first place, and how we felt during and after it. In that regard, it's never about the other guy; it's always about us.

So, now when I look at my life in the nineties through this filter, I'm quite appalled. Things started out with a bang and ended in a perceived defeat so thorough, I either needed a complete overhaul in thinking, or I needed to leave this reality. I dropped out of public life for almost six years and grappled with what I knew to be true about the nature of reality versus what I'd created, and the great gulf between.

That gulf turned out to be trust. Not trust in the Seth material, which never wavered, but in my ability to use my knowledge and intuition—you might even say to *become* my knowledge and intuition. Certainly I'd had a level of trust toward various aspects of myself during the nineties, or I would have self-destructed completely, simply because I would have created a reality devoid of trust—therefore, a reality quite literally devoid of a path forward, because that's what a total lack of trust creates.

Fortunately, I had created a middle ground for myself, believing in all aspects of the Seth material, just not trusting myself with all I knew—and it finally caught up with me. And it led me back into the material with new eyes and needs, and the emergence of changes so profound I finally experience the freedom of safety I've sought since reading my first Seth book.

And it also led me to write this book about the oft times elusive commodity called trust, and how I finally, irrevocably, found it— and how you can too, through specific Sethian knowledge and the integration and application of that knowledge. And it started with the story below.

A Wake-Up Call

In late spring of 1998, ten months before my love, my muse, my best friend Stan Ulkowski died, we'd been on the Ouija board talking to the Committee, or as they said, our inner selves, whom we had conversed with for many years. That specific session turned out to be a pivotal experience for me, although I didn't realize it at the time. It was to prepare me for what was to come, and set the direction for the rest of my life.

I started in my usual way with the Committee, which was to complain—complain about what I wanted out of life, versus what I had in life. I started rattling off things I wanted, such as satisfaction and fulfillment, and to know how to interact with the universe on a positive, quick level.

And the Committee said, "So, what do you have when you get all these things you want?" I threw out a list of responses, ending in the lofty catch-all "value fulfillment." To my surprise and consternation, they said: "No, no, no. Cut to the bottom line. What is it you really want?" When I hesitated, they said, "Look, think about this carefully. It is the foundation upon which you will build the rest of your life."

Several months went by as I studied the unresolved puzzle of what I lacked. Then, about two months before Stan passed, I was at a rest stop in Portland, Oregon, catching a quick nap on my way south to Eugene, our home of the day. As I was coming out of the dream state, but not yet fully conscious, I clearly heard the word *trust*.

And I knew then trust was the answer to my puzzle—but the answer seemed anticlimactic. Because, I thought to myself, I *do* trust. I believe with all my heart and soul in all aspects of the Seth material. I've spent years working with the material and doing my best to integrate it into my life. So, what else, I asked myself, rather naively in retrospect, was there to trust?

Life went on, and then two months later Stan suddenly died. Only those who have felt life seriously wobbling around them, and then lost an anchor in the storm, can even begin to comprehend the complete and utter pain involved, or the reality created because of it. How the most precious gift possible is to find truly solid footing under the onslaught of upheaval and emotions those inner and outer realities reflect.

But footing, I found, is hard to come by without one important ingredient—trust. Not garden variety trust, but a deep and abiding trust that all is right in the universe, that meaning and purpose run rampant, and that everything is really, truly okay, because it simply reflects the nature of reality. And because All That Is *is* everything. A trust that goes light years beyond intellectual trust and into the realm of absolutes.

And I finally saw for myself what the Committee was getting at. Without true and absolute trust, I could not live comfortably in my reality. I could not effortlessly understand the underlying psychical conditions and circumstances of all events without absolute trust and, therefore, I could not consciously create a direction I could sustain. And because of it, I could not get what I wanted out of my time in physical reality. Trust was the magnet that would automatically draw to me the fulfillment of the psyche I so sought.

So, I scoured the Seth material yet again, trying to grasp the implications of what Seth was saying, but now from a different perspective. I began to filter his words through a new prism, one aimed almost solely at helping me *become* trust.

Primary and Secondary Reversed

This probably won't seem like an earthshaking epiphany to you, but what I'd been doing that so limited my thinking and, therefore, my trust in the events I met, was seeing myself primarily as consciousness living as a human in linear time, obviously with psychic roots outside of time, but still mostly functioning within it.

As I said, no earthshaking epiphany—because that's what I am; and it's what you are too. But what I learned from Seth this time was viewing reality from that stance alone is intensely limiting. This time the Seth material led me into rethinking who I primarily am, and viewing reality from that standpoint. The material, in essence, led me to the fact that, not just theoretically, not just spiritually, but very practically, I am not primarily an ego in time; I am *primarily* a consciousness which exists in the spacious present.

And as long as I placed such a strong belief in linear time and my place in it, I would not only keep hitting the hurtful results of cause and effect thinking, I would not effectively use the tools that come with that primary territory. And, therefore, scaling the wall of trust was far more difficult, perhaps for me even impossible.

Trust in the 25th Century

In Jane Roberts' wonderful novel, *Oversoul Seven and the Museum of Time*, Seven and a rather motley group of his twentieth century aspects come together in a very odd set of circumstances.

From Oversoul Seven's broader perspective, he realizes that underlying the surface events they are all involved in is the real drama, and it's about something called the Codicils. It becomes Seven's task to figure out what the Codicils are and why they're so important, and then to secure them in time and space for future generations.

Oversoul Seven ends up fast-forwarding through time to the twenty-fifth century, where yet another of his personalities resides. This person, called Monarch, is the head of an archeological dig at which the Codicils were discovered some 200 years previously, and which had altered civilization as it was then known.

In honor of the Codicils and their tremendous impact on humanity, Monarch built a replica of a house from the nineteenth century where the Codicils were first penned—and this replicated house became a world museum which held the Codicils, and it was called the Museum of Time.

It's a wonderful story full of learning for all of us. But, for me, the most intriguing part is how Monarch's twenty-fifth century world functions. Paranoia has not been felt for decades. Crime is unknown to the people. Indeed, at one point Monarch thinks to himself that no thievery has been committed in his lifetime. He goes on to remember all social diseases have been eliminated for over a century. Monarch says the causes of such things have been done away with almost naturally, as humankind taught itself about its own potentials and abilities and, we assume, came to trust them.

Certainly we Seth readers are on that journey. We started it with our first Seth book and we've come a long way. But Monarch's world is one where the safe universe concept is a given, where it's practiced, not just accepted in theory; where a complete trust in everything important is the mode of the day, such as trust in All That Is, trust in their inner selves, trust in themselves, trust in the nature of reality.

The people of Monarch's world could not have created lives free of fear without trust, which actually is what gives the safe universe concept life and reality.

Finding the Significant Difference

Several years ago, I remember reading a line of Seth's where he says, "As you think of it, consciousness is barely—barely—half developed."[1] And I wondered, would he have said that to Monarch? Monarch saw himself not as a human consciousness in linear time, but as a nonphysical consciousness *using* linear time for his own purposes. And it was his focus on that significant difference that allowed him to live a safe universe—without disease, without fear, with clarity, with absolute trust. And it will us too.

Seeking Beyond Old Perceptions

How far along the road to unconditional trust and our own personal safe universes are we? Certainly, the basic but intricate fabric of our individual lives has changed radically over the years, thanks to the Seth material. But where, truly, are we?

Are we experiencing the level of trust we know is possible? Trust that automatically leads to positive outcomes? Or, are we still butting heads with beliefs and actions that limit the fulfillment of our lives, because we don't really trust enough to engender serious change? And if we are, why?

I had limited my trust and, therefore, my development and safety, by how I viewed what I read in the Seth material, the lens or filter I ran the material through and worked within. I'd had a complete reorientation of thinking because of the Seth material, a complete reorientation of my life. But now I needed to reorient further in order to trust more and be safe. Did I need to ask different questions to get answers that would take me beyond where I was in my thinking? You bet.

So, I went back into the Seth material on another journey, basically looking for what I had not seen before—that is, information that could expand my thinking, giving me another path to explore as I grappled with my dual physical and nonphysical stance in existence. I wasn't looking for new information per se, because I'd read and studied everything Seth has said in his books countless times. But I *was* looking for a broadening in my perspective that would allow me to understand and, therefore, trust at a new level.

And I did find that new perspective. Not quickly, and not immediately obvious to me, but there nonetheless. In time, I fully saw what I'd been doing, and how it had very much impacted my ability to unequivocally trust myself, to trust my inner self, to trust the nature of reality. And that new perspective is what I will lay out for you in this book.

A Psychic Manifesto, by Jane Roberts
(from *The God of Jane*)

My life is its own definition.
So is yours.
Let us leave the priests to their hells and heavens,
And confine the scientists to their dying universe
And accidently created stars.
Let us each dare to open our dream's door,
And explore the unofficial thresholds, where we begin.

Starting Our Search for Trust

Seth says, "When man realizes that he himself creates his personal and universal environment in concrete terms, then he can begin to create a private and universal environment much superior to the one that is a result of haphazard and unenlightened constructions. This is our main message to the world, and this is the next line in man's conceptual development, which will be felt in all fields...."[1]

Haphazard and unenlightened constructions. That's what Seth says we're creating to date, and he's talking about in our personal as well as public lives. However, he then says, "When you get to the point that you realize you are forming your day-to-day existence and the life that you know, then you can begin to alter your own mental and psychic patterns and, therefore, change your daily environment."[2] And Seth has been doing his best to help us along. He says not only has he been trying to divest us of official ideas, but to prepare us for the acceptance of a new version of reality.

So, what are the official ideas Seth is trying to divest us of so we can live this new version of reality? It's what he calls the official line of consciousness, and its main organizing factor is linear time. He says, "The official line of consciousness forms a world about it, and you perceive and experience that world, and it will always show you the results of the beliefs inherent in the official line of consciousness. While you devote yourself to that official line of consciousness, the world will always appear the same...."[3]

The reason it will always appear the same is because the official consciousness gives us no place to go, no openings to aspire to outside the limitations of linear time, because it claims there is evolution—and cause and effect—and one world—and one timeline for that world—and one timeline for us. It tells us these are facts and, therefore, cannot be altered. They just *are*. And those facts force us to think a certain way, a way that leaves little to no room to believe or trust we, as Seth says, create our personal and universal environments in concrete terms.

The good news, according to Seth, is this: "The one-line stage of consciousness was necessary.... But that stage contained within it its own impetus. It set up challenges that could not be solved at that stage of consciousness, and that would automatically lead you into other strands of awareness. Only then can those contradictions make sense. Only then can you say, individually—and listen now—'I live in a safe universe.'"[4]

Some of those challenges Seth's talking about take the form of our haphazard and unenlightened constructions, all created by our lack of trust in our inherent safety in the universe. In order to solve our issues made manifest in those constructions, we need to become aware of other information, and then think differently because of it.

Understanding Real Time

Years ago I read a line from Seth I didn't understand, and it puzzled me for a long while. He says, "Your ideas of time are detrimental. ... Time works with you and not against you."[5] (He told Rob to underline it four times.) And the more I read the Seth material, it finally hit me that Seth was probably talking about two different kinds of time in that one statement.

When he says, "Your ideas of time are detrimental," I think he's talking about our ideas of linear time and our acceptance of cause and effect—which is what linear time is all about, and from which come our beliefs that we're all alone and without any consciously controllable safety. And when Seth says, "Time works with you and not against you," I think he's talking about subjective time working with us, subjective time in the spacious present—which is the only real time there is, according to him, and from which comes the *reason* for our controllable safety.

And it struck me that if we can get a grip on the use of subjective time, then time truly will work for us, mostly because we will drop the idea of cause and effect. By dropping the idea of cause and effect, we will significantly change the rules of the game. Seth says, "As you understand time, you will eventually be able to merge your inner comprehension with your physical self, and form your world on a conscious basis. Such manuscripts as mine are meant to help you do precisely that."[6]

Indeed, time is the issue. We need a different perspective on time, an expansion of our thinking to include the working assumption that time is subjective, not objective; therefore, we can override the belief in cause and effect.

And why would we care to do this? Because understanding the subjective nature of time is the key to living a safe universe, one without haphazard constructions, one lived in trust. And it is perhaps one of the most difficult issues for us to grasp. Not theoretically or intellectually, because we can pretty much understand what Seth is saying about simultaneous time vs. linear time, or at least we can see the outlines of the bigger picture. That's not where our issue lies.

The real challenge in understanding and using time to our advantage lies in the fact we believe linear time. Not that we believe *in* it—but we *believe* it! That is, we believe it when we assume an action we took yesterday caused an event today. We believe it when a memory of a "past" event is accepted as a concrete, finished part of our past. We believe it when something happens to us in the present we accept as a random event. We believe it when an object is assumed to be solid. We believe it when we assume there is something beyond the walls of our home, always there even if we don't see it.

Some ideas about linear time we've loosened. When we no longer fear death, we've loosened the hold of linear time. When we know the illness or accident we experienced was caused by us, we've loosened the hold of linear time. When we consciously choose a lucid dream or an out of body experience, we've loosened the hold of linear time. But, overall, a belief in linear time dominates our lives. And yet—and this is the ironic part—we know our rock solid view of linear time and cause and effect is a detriment to us and to our individual growth, because it doesn't lead us to trust and safety; that our freedom lies in understanding and using simultaneous time.

Seth says, "You have put yourselves in a position where your consciousness must now become aware of the probable pasts and probable futures, in order to form for yourselves a sane, fulfilling, and creative present."[7] And we can't accept or work with the probabilities surrounding pasts, presents and futures, and the implications of it all, unless we truly accept and work with subjective time.

So, this book is in direct response to one of the challenges Seth has laid down for us—paraphrased, to loosen our hold on linear time thinking, because our efforts will lead us to freedom from haphazard and unenlightened constructions, and into a sane and fulfilling present based in trust. In other words, into a safe universe.

Using Another Kind of Time

What we will do herein is to frame our realities through the lens of simultaneous time instead of linear time. In order to do that, we have to start from a different place than our thinking normally takes us. That is, instead of seeing and discussing our lives as emerging from linear time, and trying to use that framework to bring about change, we will see our realities as immersed in the spacious present in subjective time, and learn to use the knowledge and tools of that framework.

Seth said to Jane and Rob, and it applies to all of us: "You recognized the overall <u>vitality</u> of our material—but you did not realize that it meant a complete reorientation of your attitudes. You did not realize that you were being presented, not merely with an alternate view of reality, but with the closest approximation you could get of what reality was, and how it worked, and what it meant."[8]

And reality is not linear time and cause and effect. To get to a complete reorientation of our attitudes, we can't just theoretically accept Seth's wonderful alternate view of reality. We really must bring it alive in our thinking, which will quite literally bring it alive in our present. We need to own it as our bedrock platform of thought, not just as an intriguing but abstract idea of Seth's. We must make it ours.

So, that became my personal task; and what quickly followed that commitment was the realization I couldn't hold absolute trust without utter faith in the universe's intent first. I needed to fully understand *why and how* the universe leans in my direction, as Seth says it does, and I needed to know it happens constantly and with superlative intent. I needed to see that goodness and support were always mine, and could only seem dulled through troubled eyes. And to have that kind of faith, I had to ultimately know more about All That Is.

So, my search for trust took me once more to the beginning, which by definition is All That Is. And that is what the underlying theme of this book is all about, no matter the subject under discussion at the time. It's about All That Is, which means it's about consciousness, which means it's about you and me. And it's about how All That Is creates and why, which means it's about how consciousness creates and why; therefore, how you and I create and why. So, when I now say this book is all about you and me, there's no contradiction here.

Living a Safe Universe Vs. Living *In* a Safe Universe

Before we go further into a book with a title like this one, an explanation is needed. Seth says, "You live in a safe universe. This is not only a valid psychic truth, but is the basis for cellular integrity."[9] All That Is is of good intent, and everything created is within All That Is, which means it can only be of good intent. Consciousness expands through value fulfillment, which is equivalent to growth in physical reality. And value fulfillment allows for the creation of all possible manifestations, with the purpose being to learn and grow from one's own manifestations. So, while we live *in* a very safe universe, our manifestations can make it seem unsafe; and therein lies the difference between living *in* a safe universe and living one.

To be safe means we must come to understand how our manifestations come into being, not from the false perspective of linear time/cause and effect, but from the true perspective of consciousness in the spacious present. And to do that, we'll start by offering certain topics in chapters of their own; and then we'll tie the concepts together through examples and methods of application. But never forget when you're reading this, in the end it all comes together under one umbrella, the umbrella of All That Is.

One point to make here: As Seth readers, we know of the complexity of his multilayered ideas. Nothing he says is one-dimensional, a simple sentence or two to be taken at face value, as is so much in the New Age. "You create your own reality," for instance, spawns book after book of Seth's, because it starts with All That Is and ends up in the lap of each of us, with all bases discussed along the way. It's the story of the workings of the mighty universe, as complete, complex and eye-opening as is currently found in this reality.

Which is my way of saying, don't expect any subject I bring up to be complete, in Seth's terms. As I walked my personal path to trust, I felt as though I was following crumbs at times, looking for the next logical step, the next bit of information that would pull together a picture of creation meaningful to me that would lead to psychological trust, the only trust there is; something that coalesced into a body of work I could finally grab on to and say, "Now I clearly see how it works, this thing called creation." And to get there, I needed to see a subject from the point of what it would do for me in securing my path, not in all its implications to the universe overall.

So, I narrowed my focus and eventually winnowed down to the subjects, or picture, explained in this book. You will not find this summary anywhere in the Seth material. You will find much more than I write on any given subject, and you will find topics that could tie in with a broader redefinition of the self that I chose not to write about, such as the inner senses and dreams, because they didn't come into play in my search for trust. But you will not find my chosen subjects in the order presented, or even with the logical conclusions that draw them together as I did in my mind.

It is my sincerest hope that in this condensed version of creation I present, you will find freedom to trust, freedom to truly live a safe universe. And to get there, we must, as Jane Roberts says in her Psychic Manifesto, explore the unofficial thresholds where we begin.

2

There is a portion of All That Is directed and focused within each individual, residing within each consciousness. Each consciousness is, therefore, cherished and individually protected.
—*Seth,* The Seth Material, *Chapter 18*

All That Is

All of the Seth material is fascinating to me, and I found chapter one in *Dreams, "Evolution," and Value Fulfillment* especially meaningful, as my search for trust kicked off. It's titled "Before the Beginning," and is, of course, about All That Is. More specifically it's about how and why all creation happens, and how and why physical reality emerges from the creativity of All That Is.

To set the stage—because without this particular stage nothing in this book will make final sense—I give you Seth: "The universe will begin yesterday. The universe began tomorrow. Both of these statements are quite meaningless. The tenses are wrong, and perhaps your time sense is completely outraged. Yet the statement, 'The universe began in some distant past,' is, in basic terms, just as meaningless.... The universe is being created <u>now</u>."[1]

This concept is so significant it will drive all points made herein. But because of the need to communicate in understandable terms, the words past, present and future, and variations thereof, must be allowed their limited due.

What we're about to discuss is the information, in my opinion, that has the distinction of differentiating the Seth material from any other body of work in today's world. This is the information that sets Seth head and shoulders apart and finally makes sense of everything else, in both a logical as well as an intuitive way, because it describes the very core of the self.

A Triumphant Breakthrough

Before the beginning of physical reality, Seth says All That Is—which he also calls divine subjectivity, infinite subjectivity and original subjectivity, among other terms—existed as an omnipotent creative source which contained within itself an infinity of all possible creations. These creations came into vivid being within the subjectivity of All That Is through its slightest imagining, dream, thought, feeling and mood. And All That Is was "divinely astonished" by the vitality and brilliance of those thoughts and imaginings, and All That Is knew they inherited from it the ability themselves to create.

In its divine astonishment, All That Is began *listening* to its mental progeny, listening to what they wanted, while noting the interactions which occurred amongst them. And, for the first time, All That Is began to respond to its progeny.

With this development, All That Is started feeling a growing sense of pressure. It was realizing its own ever-multiplying thoughts and dreams, its progeny, yearned to enjoy their endowed and innate gift of creativity fully, more so than simply creating their own mental progeny. They wanted more. They wanted something completely unheard of. What they wanted was *a unique state of being.*

And All That Is became possessed by the need to lovingly transform its own reality in such a way all of its mental progeny could, indeed, come into a wholly unique state of being. Through previously unimaginable leaps of divine inspiration, All That Is then saw that freedom through *objectivity* was the way to give all of its progeny the path to deeper creative fulfillment. A door needed to open which would allow the progeny of All That Is to experience a seeming outer reality that would emerge from, yet be contained within, the inner realm of All That Is.

With that massive divine inspiration, All That Is saw in a flash what mental conditions would be needed to create worlds which mirrored the feelings and desires of consciousness—*all* consciousness, because within All That Is was every consciousness which would ever manifest into an objective reality, and they all yearned for deeper expression.

As All That Is saw those mental conditions, it imagined those worlds, and in a monumental explosive flash they were created. They were taken out of subjectivity and into objectivity. All That Is, within and as its progeny, was finally free to *fully* experience. As Seth says, it was the *triumphant breakthrough into another kind of being.*

We are the progeny of All That Is, existing objectively yet still within All That Is, because we wanted it and All That Is wanted it *as us.* We *are* All That Is.

Action

Our desire at times is to spiritualize the wonders of All That Is, to throw up our hands and say, it's simply beyond me, this miracle of creation, and see it as a gauzy awesomeness beyond our comprehension. But there is a pattern of logic that permeates everything, a logic we can work with, but it takes more understanding of how All that Is creates.

Before objectified reality, when the only reality expression was subjective, all things—identities, realities, objects—were already created and held subjectively and simultaneously within All That Is. They simply were not materialized, or objectified, within the subjective reality of All That Is.

But, even after objective reality (what we call, in our case, physical reality) was created by All That Is within and as an extension of its subjectivity, not all of All That Is can ever be fully objectified, part of it always has to be remain subjective. But it's a pressing desire on the part of All That Is to continually objectify, or materialize, some of itself, so there is a constant attempt to do so. And this attempt, this trying, results in action. Not the action of motion as we know it, but the action of All That Is. Seth says, "Action is the breath of inner vitality (*of All That Is*), of which all materializations of any kind are composed. It represents the relationship between unexpressed inner vitality and materialized vitality."[2] Some might call it creation.

So action, or the breath of inner vitality, begins from within All That Is, and is a part of All That Is. And since action is a part of

All That Is, the materializations which occur because of this action are, simply put, All That Is expressing itself in different forms.

Which means everything that's materialized in whatever reality, in whatever form, is All That Is lovingly expressing itself as action. There is nothing anywhere, ever, which is not All That Is expressing itself as action...and that includes as us.

The Three Creative Dilemmas of All That Is

To explain all this further, Seth talks about three creative dilemmas which occur because of the constant need of All That Is to keep creation happening, or said another way, to keep action happening, because creation and action are one. And while this won't seem so obvious at first, the dilemmas are the birthplace of everything, which is why they're so important to us and our trek through the creation process.

The first creative dilemma is actually what we've already talked about. Here's how Seth words it: "The first creative dilemma is that which exists when inner vitality struggles to completely materialize, though it cannot completely materialize."[3]

This constant struggle results in action. But this struggle is not only the birth of action, it's the birth of identities. Seth says, "An identity is also a dimension of existence, action within action, an unfolding of action upon itself; and through this interweaving of action with itself, an identity is formed."[4]

Yet, although identity is formed from action, action and identity cannot be separated. So, an identity *is* action. And what identities are Seth talking about? He's saying any identity that ever comes into being starts here. Nowhere in the greatest stretches of All That Is, expressed and not expressed, is there a mechanism other than action which creates identities. And that becomes a key factor when we later start talking about ourselves and our personal realities, and it brings great clarity to those subjects.

Every identity starts existence right here during the first creative dilemma, lovingly created and safely supported by All That Is.

The second creative dilemma, interestingly, teaches us about the beginnings of consciousness. Seth says the second dilemma occurs because identity, because of its characteristics, continually seeks stability, while stability is impossible. And he adds, "It is this dilemma, precisely between identity's constant attempts to maintain stability, and action's inherent drive for change, that results in the imbalance, the exquisite creative by-product that is consciousness of <u>self</u>."[5]

So, the second dilemma brings consciousness into this process. Entities (which we'll talk about in a later chapter) are formed from this stage of the three dilemmas. They are the conscious portion of identities, gestalt patterns of perception by which action knows itself. And entities constantly change, because each action causes another action, which causes change.

A note here: You may have noticed Seth didn't say consciousness comes first and then identities are formed from consciousness—which is the prevailing idea in the New Age. All That Is is *conscious*, but *it is not consciousness*. So, the knowledge that identities come before consciousness breaks Seth apart from other works, and finally relieves the need to dress consciousness in spiritual clothes, similar to God's but now called New Age. What Seth says is consciousness is a tool simply used by identities. He also says consciousness is the direction in which the self looks at any given time.

The third creative dilemma described by Seth is when consciousness of self, created in the second dilemma, attempts to separate itself from action, resulting in a state of ego.

So, consciousness of self is not the same as consciousness of *ego* self, which is, of course, what we are. Seth says, "Ego consciousness involves a state in which consciousness of self attempts to divorce itself from action, an attempt on the part of consciousness to perceive action as an object."[6]

Ego consciousness views action, or All That Is, as though action is outside itself manifested into standalone objects, including its own body and everything in its environment. It sees action as a *result* rather than a *cause* of its existence and experience and, therefore, attempts to control it. But separation between action and ego consciousness, or ego consciousness and objects, is obviously impossible, since no consciousness or identity can exist without action, because they are inseparable. So, when ego gives up its hold on what it considers control of action, it opens the action field to the point where almost any action is possible.

And one point here. From All That Is to action to identity to consciousness is actually all one loop of continuing action within simultaneous time and with no separation. So, as ego consciousness, we are simply All That Is—action and identity and consciousness of self—attempting to divorce our self and our materialized objects from action, and not actually able to do so. This whole issue becomes paramount to us understanding we *are* All That Is, not an offshoot, not a consciousness formed and placed in a reality of separation.

Reviewing the Three Creative Dilemmas

1. The first dilemma is when the inner vitality of All That Is struggles to completely materialize, but it can't completely materialize, and that attempt results in action and then identities, and they are integrated and inseparable. And each action terminates the previous action, it does not build upon it, which means an identity is also terminated with each action, and re-created with each "subsequent" action.

2. The second dilemma happens because identity constantly attempts to maintain stability, but action, which is always integrated with identity, has an inherent drive for change; and that imbalance between the two results in what Seth calls "the exquisite creative by-product which is consciousness of self."

3. The third dilemma is when consciousness of self attempts to separate itself from action and see itself, and everything else around it, as objects, resulting in a state of ego.

Seth says, "These three dilemmas represent three areas within which inner reality, or inner vitality, can experience itself."[7] And he adds the creative dilemmas are the basis for all realities, and the heart of all meaning.

Snapshot Review of Consciousness

To bring consciousness home in a more condensed view, I offer you some of the basic ideas, highlighted here:

* All That Is is <u>conscious,</u> but <u>it is not consciousness.</u>

* All That Is creates *all* identities.

* Consciousness, which is action that is conscious of itself, is created for each identity.

* Our entities (and, by extension, our inner selves) are the <u>result</u> of consciousness of self being part of an identity.

* When consciousness of self attempts to divorce itself from action, seeing action as an object, the process creates ego consciousness—which is what we are.

* So, we are *<u>action which is conscious of itself,</u>* perceiving action as objects (tables, bodies, cats, etc.).

Action's Characteristics

To help clarify action, and how and why it works as it does, I offer you these further chosen tidbits on the subject.

* Action takes place in the spacious present.

* Each action terminates the previous action.

* Without termination, no new action on the part of the identity would be possible.

* And that is why action can never complete itself—action <u>always</u> involves change.

* Action is a dimension of existence, an unfolding of action upon itself.

* An identity exists within the action in its dimension of existence.

* Without action, an identity could not continue to be conscious, because it would not be renewed—it would terminate.

* A thought is action, as is a dream.

* Action is a part of any reality, and at the same time a by-product of reality.

* Each action creates a new reality.

* Action materializes in all camouflage forms.

* Since each action terminates the previous action, linear time is simply our brain's perception of continuous action slowed down and drawn out.

This is it, folks. This is how and why creation happens. And nothing happens outside these three dilemmas, because the dilemmas constitute how All That Is lovingly creates. First action, then identities, then consciousnesses, then realities, then objects— everything happens right here. And accepting the fact we are not primarily human consciousness in linear time, but wholly non-physical consciousness within All That Is in subjective time, changes the ground rules completely, because we know where we start and how and why we create. We know *all consciousness creates the same way*, because it is the way All That Is creates.

But the changed ground rules have to be recognized, and built upon, in order to effectively lead us to a personal safe universe— one without doubt, without fear, with clarity, with absolute trust. And knowing this and other things we'll discuss in the following chapters, we will come to see how to use that knowledge to create our realities more consciously, without haphazard and unenlightened constructions.

A note before moving on: Much of the information on action and the three creative dilemmas is found in *The Early Sessions, Books 3 and 4*. They are well worth your read.

3

You must simply and practically try to divest yourself of all ideas of time as you know it.... Basically what you can time does not exist. I am trying to tell you what does exist instead.
— Seth, The Early Sessions, Book 9, *Session 429*

The Spacious Present

Seth tells us, "You need not say, 'The universe is safe,' for at your present level, that will only enrage you! You say, instead, 'I live in a safe universe,' and so you shall."[1]

When all is said and done, what we really want out of this existence is to live a personal safe universe, isn't it? That is, we want to live without doubt, without fear, with clarity and with absolute trust, because with that psychic platform under us, our creative bases are covered. No more haphazard and unenlightened constructions that seem out of our control, but instead constructions that mirror back satisfaction and our innate understanding and use of the nature of reality.

And an interesting thing happens along the way to a safe universe. We redefine our self. Indeed, we cannot get from here to there without that redefinition in place, because we can't create overall safety without understanding *why* safety is even possible.

And that *why* is answered only through an expanded understanding of the self. And the self cannot be redefined, or even understood, without ultimately understanding more about All That is and its spacious present.

Continuing the Redefinition of the Self

Seth says, "The matter of time is highly important if you have any hopes of understanding the self in its entirety."[2] Why is that? Why would understanding time help us understand ourselves better? Because the concept of the spacious present, with its simultaneous time—which Seth says is the only sort of time that has any real meaning, blows to hell and gone the boundaries imposed by linear time thinking. In one fell swoop, we break out of that official line of consciousness Seth talks about, and move our minds to a whole new way of organizing our thoughts and, therefore, our realities.

Normally, we see ourselves living a timeline from birth to death, residing on terra firma and watching as the moments pass into days, and then into months and years. Our past seems firm and tidy, a true and unchanging picture of where we've been; and our future awaits us, replete with discrete events that will happen to us, mostly outside our control. Here we reside, human beings physically separated from everything and everybody by space and time.

That picture tightly defines us and our boundaries. Before we even take into additional consideration the psychological and physical aspects of ourselves, we've acceded to that basic definition of self. And as long as we agree with that definition, we cannot live a safe universe, because along with that definition, honed by a belief in space and time, comes cause and effect. And along with a belief in cause and effect come haphazard and unenlightened constructions, created out of fear and worry and doubt and guilt (among other things).

But, thankfully, there's hope for us yet, and it comes with understanding the spacious present. Seth says, "When the spacious present is understood, with its attributes of spontaneity, then the cause and effect theory will fall. The cause and effect theory being the result of continuity holds no water."[3]

All That Is and the Spacious Present

So far in our redefinition of the self, we've learned we are consciousness that comes/came into being because of the action of All That Is. To continue expanding on that definition, we need to learn more about All That Is, since it is our basis. And that brings us squarely to the spacious present, because the spacious present, with its simultaneous time, is the infinite psychological canvas upon which All That Is creates.

This canvas of the infinite mind, this spacious present, is not separate from All That Is but a part of it. It is where all action, or creation, takes place. It is where all probabilities are found in all of their infinite, alive and expanding possibilities, each one created through a mental action of All That Is during the three creative dilemmas (which, you'll recall, is the only way creation happens). And nothing ever leaves this psychological state of All That Is, or the spacious present, because there is nowhere else to go, since nothing exists outside of All That Is and its simultaneous time.

Since everything is created in all of its infinite patterns and forms in the spacious present, it clearly means all identities and objects reside in the spacious present in past, present and future probabilities. Seth nails the idea down with this: "In the spacious present...all things that have existed still exist, and all things that shall exist in your tomorrow already do exist."[4]

Okay, so what does this mean for the redefinition of the self? It's the blockbuster idea that since each of us is an ongoing action of All That Is, we create in the spacious present by default. There is no subset of creation that can happen anywhere else—it is an impossibility. To emphasize and clarify, *no creation can happen unless it takes place in the spacious present in simultaneous time.*

So, no matter where the self *thinks* it resides (i.e. linear time), it can only reside in the spacious present. Seth says, "You are in the spacious present now. You were in the spacious present in your yesterday, and you will not have traveled through it in your tomorrow, or eons of tomorrows."[5] Any other time scheme used by consciousness is simply camouflage constructed within the spacious present.

So, what does this mean to our accepted, unquestioned belief in a past, present and future, or linear time? Not so much. Seth says, "To look backward into the past entails looking forward into the future, and there is no firm ground, you see; there is no present in a basic manner, no firm ground that is the present, from which to view the future or the past. For they are all one, and you are a part of the spacious present."[6]

To briefly recap before we move on to the implications of camouflage in the spacious present, keep in mind the spacious present is a part of All That Is, as is everything else. It's where all action takes place, which means it's where all identities and probabilities and realities and objects are formed, and re-formed, within simultaneous time, and continually exist. Nothing ever leaves the spacious present, including us. Seth says there is no place to go, then adds rather enigmatically, there are as many places to go as we wish to find. Which is an intriguing point, and one which will later be seen to be a very important part of our emerging platform of trust and clarity.

Creating Camouflage in the Spacious Present

Did you know when hurtling down the highway at 80 miles an hour, you're not going anywhere? When flying at 30,000 feet, you're not moving through space? As you progress from birth to death, you have not physically grown? When 100 people view a room, 100 rooms are created? To clarify and explore these statements, we'll take a look at how our individual camouflage realities are created in the spacious present, and we'll learn many things about the self along the way.

First, though, we need to clear up what a reality is and where it exists. Seth says identity and its action is a dimension of existence; and that the reality of an identity exists within the action and cannot be separated from it. So, realities exist within the identity/action's dimension of existence, not alone or separate from the identity, shuffled off somewhere outside of it. And the ego consciousness (personality), being a portion of the identity, isn't plopped down *outside of itself* and told to go create. Since realities are a *part* of identity/action, they cannot be separated from an identity, and nothing in a reality can be called not-self, because the self is the *whole* of the action.

When dropped to the bottom line, this says I have my reality and you have yours, but we do not share realities per se, because I'm always in my own identity/action's dimension of existence, as we learned in the three dilemmas, and you are always in yours. *(A note: We're using identity here to suggest entity and, by extension, inner self, but there's much more to an identity than just that. We won't be talking about it in this book, though.)*

While you and I don't share realities, what we do share is the ability in the spacious present to communicate telepathically. And this ability to telepathically communicate allows us to agree on similarities between our realities. For instance, those of us who are reading this page agree we live in a specific year in a world generally known to us to have certain characteristics of culture, countries, languages, etc. I may never visit a city called Paris, but I know it exists in the overall agreement made between us.

And because of that agreement, I basically form my reality to coincide with yours. But since you are not actually in my reality, and cannot be, because you are within your own dimension of existence, the objects I see cannot be seen by you, nor can yours be seen by me. As Seth says to Jane and Rob and a friend of theirs, "Each of the three of you creates your own glass, in your own personal perspective. Therefore you have three different physical glasses here, but each one exists in an entirely different space continuum."[7]

And what's as stunning is that you hold an idea construction of what you look like, and what I create in my reality is a rendition of your idea construction of yourself. The original idea construction of you is always yours, though, and as you change it, I update my reality to coincide with yours.

To drive this point home to its ultimate conclusion: We can never be anywhere but in our own unique reality, and that reality, as, and because of, action can *only* exist in the spacious present. So, here I exist in the spacious present within my identity, creating a camouflage reality for my own needs and purposes; and you do likewise in yours.

Setting the Framework for a Time and Space Reality

In order to experience the idea of linear time in my dimension of existence, I "first" construct the framework of a space/time continuum, because space and time are the defining parameters of linear time. But the space/time continuum is camouflage, of course, even though camouflage with great purpose.

So, I now pretend to "live" in my camouflage reality with everything contingent on my root assumptions, or beliefs, in linear time and space (ergo, the space/time continuum). But I'm really in the spacious present with continuous terminations of the previous action by the current one, as we learned in the first creative dilemma. How, then, do I hold it all together, this illusion of continuity in time and space, when there is no continuity there, ever?

According to Seth, a complete physical reality is re-created millions of times a second, as one action terminates the one before it. So, millions of times a second, everything we see is terminated and re-created, with a new version of everything we see and touch, including our bodies. And an important point—each new action is different than the previously terminated one, even if only subtly, because no action can be identical to another. Remember, action is creation, and each creation by All That Is is unique—a point we will return to again and again.

The Camouflage of Duration in Time, and Matter in Space

So, here we are, consciousness in our own camouflage reality within the spacious present, defining a space/time continuum to create the illusion of space and time. Let's look at some of the underlying truths to that situation then, and we'll better come to understand, of all things, the self.

Since there is no time, and since each action terminates the previous action, it means there is no duration to anything we see. As Seth tells us, "Matter of itself, however, is no more continuous, no more given to growth or age than is, say, the color yellow."[8] To hone that idea further, Seth says, "Matter is continually created, but no particular object is in itself continuous. There is not, for example, one physical object that deteriorates with age. There are instead continuous creations of psychic energy into a physical pattern that appears to hold a more or less rigid appearance."[9]

And with each creation, millions of times a second, the object changes, because *action is change*. In a camouflage reality with its root assumptions of time and space, very gradual change looks like development, or aging and wear. But a muscleman cannot grow muscles by working out through time, in a medium of space, because neither exists. And without time and space, there can be no *motion*. Seth said earlier when discussing the spacious present, there is no place to go, and the reason is because no motion can occur unless there is both time and space—and, again, neither exists. Seth elaborates on this point by saying since both space and time are camouflages, to speak of traveling through them is meaningless.

How does one walk across the room, then, or drive to the grocery store, without time or space? How does a muscleman develop muscles without time and space in which to grow them? Those are questions answered in the chapter on suggestion. For now, just lock on to the idea that since there is no time or space, nothing is around long enough to grow or age, or materially expand.

The Purpose of the Camouflage Brain

An important point to consider here is this: If there is no time and no space, leading to no duration of matter and no motion, how do we create the *illusion* of being in a continuous reality one day at a time, surrounded by objects? First, the mind always resides in the spacious present, but the brain is part of the camouflage of a physical reality. And the brain has a very specific purpose. Its neuronal structure creates that illusion of time and space for us, and its perceptive mechanisms of sight, touch, smell, taste and hearing point the inner portion of I to do the actual conversion of action into objects.

Which means this: If we cannot see, touch, smell, taste or hear something, it does not exist in our camouflage reality. It always exists in the spacious present, of course, but not within our personal camouflage reality.

So, when you walk from one room to another, does the room you exited exist in your physical reality? No. When you stand on the beach viewing the blue ocean, do the cliffs behind you exist in your reality? No. Does anything under the surface of the ocean exist in your reality? No. Only once you lay eyes on it will it exist, and then only that portion you can see. Or touch or smell or taste or hear. So, the portion of your reality that's created when your sight is out of commission (eyes closed or blind) is only what the other senses pick up. Your feet touch the sand, so the feel of your feet and the sand immediately under your feet is created, but not whatever is right next to that bit of sand upon which you stand. And when you hear your child's voice from a far room, the child is not created in your physical reality, only its voice.

And this inevitably raises the question of the creation of one fully formed *physical* world. Is there such a thing? No. How can there be? What one pair of eyes would be able to see the whole world at once, thereby bringing it fully into camouflage reality? Obviously, none.

You see, we each *are* our own dimension of existence, and our individual reality is created within it. And since we reside in the spacious present, that's the only place a camouflage reality can play out. And the spacious present has no time and no space, ergo no growth, no age, no motion. So, methods of recognizing camouflage are built into the camouflage itself, through the camouflage brain.

I think Seth rounds out nicely the ideas we've been examining here with these quotes: "As I have said that the walls of your house do not actually exist as such, so the time divisions that you have placed within the spacious present do not exist."[10] And, "Beneath all camouflage exists that which has no need of camouflage, but simply is."[11]

Leaping Forward

Let's close this chapter with what we must all attempt to do if we truly want to redefine our self to the point where we can live a safe universe. And, of course, the answer comes from Seth: "Leap over the tradition of time's framework and sense with the united intellect and intuitions your own individual part in a spacious present that is large enough to contain all of time's segments."[12]

Please don't forget, though, all of this book's subjects, as a whole, work together to help redefine the self. So, while action and identity and the spacious present are crucial to understand because of the stage they set, there's still much more to take into consideration.

4

Each consciousness impresses the universe in its own fashion. Its very existence sets up a kind of significance, in whose light the rest of the universe will be interpreted. The universe knows itself through such significances.
  —*Seth,* The Nature of the Psyche, *Session 788*

Significances

As you know by now, one of the purposes of this book is to help redefine or broaden our definition of self. And it isn't just an interesting, but ultimately impractical, exercise we're undertaking. What we're attempting to do is live a safe universe, aren't we? By definition, it suggests we've found ways to seriously lessen the frequency, strength and duration of haphazard and unenlightened constructions in our individual camouflage realities, and to increase experience of more pleasant events. And if we continue to accept our self as locked in linear time/cause and effect, then we're missing the key to freedom.

So, the plan here is to work from the top down, so to speak. We're not starting with our supposed place in linear time as our baseline, with its unquestioned acceptance of cause and effect, and then attempting to create a safe universe within all the distortions that come with that strongly held belief—and the impotence and hopelessness that many times accompany it. What we're attempting to do is to redefine the self by starting where the self starts— with All That Is—and working "down" to camouflage reality instead of "up" from it, thereby recognizing our accurate, if seldom acknowledged, abilities as consciousness. And why would we undertake this not insignificant task? Because we'll free our self from seeing our self embroiled in camouflage restrictions which have no bearing whatsoever on how creation happens—unless we believe in them. We'll see and accept the bigger, far more invigorating and accurate picture of the self.

In the previous chapter, the spacious present was the topic, and you'll recall Seth said, "In the spacious present...all things that have existed still exist, and all things that shall exist in your tomorrow already do exist." Remember, all action happens in the spacious present and stays there, it's where we reside—being action ourselves—and where we create and experience our camouflage physical realities.

Okay, we get that the spacious present holds everything that has existed or will ever exist, and we get that Seth's talking about for all consciousness at once, not one spacious present for you and one for me, with a neat package of personal possibilities held within each of them. Now we add to that another of the many consistencies found in Seth's material, and it is that there is no chaos in creation—everything happens with purpose and intent.

Which must eventually then beg the question: How does any one consciousness gather to it a range of events it can experience in its present state of being, events which meet its purpose—open ended as that may be—when the spacious present is awash in the infinite actions of *all* consciousness? The answer is a framework of enormous import is built into the spacious present as its organizing arm, a framework which draws each consciousness toward its personal defining parameters for a given existence.

And what is this all-purpose divine framework used by All That Is to keep its creations organized? It's called significances.

The Guiding Hand of Significances

In *The Nature of the Psyche*, session 788, Seth tells us, "The universe, by whatever name and in whatever manifestation, attains its reality through ordered sequences of significances." And, "You imprint the universe with your own significance, and using that as a focus you draw from it, or attract, those events that fit your unique purposes and needs." And, "Each consciousness is endowed with creativity...using its own significance as a focus to draw into its experience whatever events are possible for it from the universe itself."

Said another way, significances are a tool used by consciousness to organize the spacious present, defining from an unpredictable field of action a predictable range of action accessible to it. Although there are many ways, great and small, that the universe can be organized into predictable ranges of action, here's one example.

I am a consciousness which chose to be born as a white female living in twenty-first century America ("I" to be identified as current personality and its inner self later in the book). I chose those conditions pre-birth, with great purpose and intent behind my decisions, and I also chose certain personality and character traits. Those on-purpose choices would then act as significance magnets in the spacious present, which would define my range of potential action. Logically, that means there are significances that don't fit within what I want to experience in this particular existence. So, the significances I initially chose, which broadly define the probabilities I can experience in this lifetime, set the framework for the decisions and choices available to me.

But Seth goes on to say more about significances, clarifying for us they not only define the larger picture of our potentials in life, but also the day-to-day manifestations. In other words, *all* manifestations, large and small, start life as significances that order themselves into a meaningful array, no matter whether we're of Seth's vintage or involved in the camouflage of physical reality. Significances are used by all consciousness to bring order and boundaries, however loose they may be, to their potential creations. So, it's accurate to say all the events we meet are built of significances.

Significances, Action and Mental Acts

For those of us attempting to bring some conscious input to our creative process, here's the million dollar question: How does physical consciousness select certain significances over others in its predictable range of possibilities? It's done through the action of mental acts—thought, emotion, imagination and dreams. These actions point toward significances which match the mental acts' level of intensity and purpose.

What these mental acts do, then, is highlight significances that mean something to us in our current circumstances, and those significances change as we shift our thinking. And with each shift in thinking, the camouflage reality we're creating from significances (for that is exactly where it comes from) shifts.

Which brings us to a new definition of continuity.

Significances and Subjective Continuity

Seth says, "You understand the cause-and-effect kind of order, but (physical reality) is built upon the non-causal aspect of significances."[1] To us, continuity implies one thing happening before or after another, but Seth is saying continuity has nothing to do with a linear process. It is, in fact, formed subjectively. That is, movement within significances is based on the mental acts of consciousness, which are, by nature, subjective. Those mental acts, as discussed, are thought, emotion, imagining and dreams. They are also action, which, by action's definition, means they reorganize and constantly change the continuity of our existence, because all happenings are simultaneous and all action causes change.

And all of this is the polar opposite of cause and effect. Our realities are not created in a linear fashion, but instead through the action within mental processes. In other words, linear time has nothing to do with what we experience, or in what order. It simply acts like a framework within which we can experience the illusion of a lifeline.

To bring home this idea of no linear time, Seth says, "There is no cause and effect in the terms that you understand the words. Nor is there a succession of moments that follow one after the other, and without a succession of moments following one after the other you can see that the idea of cause and effect becomes meaningless. An action in the present cannot be based on or caused by an action in the past, and neither action can be the cause of a future action in a basic reality where neither past nor future exists."[2] And this is why Seth says when the spacious present is truly understood, the cause and effect theory will fall.

Here's an example of how subjective continuity works in Seth's experience. When he's sitting in his renowned study with a glass of brandy at hand, it's because he consciously chose that setting, detail by detail, from other significances in his overall field of significances. And when he changes his mind and wishes to experience a different ambience, he shifts immediately to a new set of mental acts, which draw new significances reflecting what he now has chosen to experience—and none of this has anything to do with cause and effect. And our subjective continuity works the same way as Seth's, because it's an identical process for all consciousness.

To clarify, significances must have the flexibility to come together in different groupings, based on changing mental acts. Since nothing is stagnant within All That Is due to action's constant forcing of change, this is a necessity, this ability to move a significance to another grouping based on a change in mental acts, a change of mind. And, in our case, because of our camouflage of linear time, the groupings have to seem as though they fall naturally in time. But they do not.

Can we be told more clearly linear time may not be the basket in which to place all our eggs? If our realities are organized by significances highlighted in the spacious present through our thoughts, imaginations, emotions and dreams, and there quite literally is *never* an objective continuity where, by default, one event and moment follows its predecessor, then it seems clear a reorganization in the way we approach reality is called for. And, as I've said before, that is what this book is all about.

Continuing to Redefine the Self

We learned about linear time because we live it. And Seth tells us much more about how we function within it. But it was only his lead-in to a completely different recognition of ourselves, so we can, as he says, learn to form our world on a *conscious* basis. And he's saying we cannot do it by accepting as ours a position in linear time, a position which concretely defines us as a physical being, first and foremost.

None of what's mentioned so far in this book is outside the self. Not action, not dimensions of existence, not identities, not the spacious present or significances or realities. One cannot exist without all the others, because, in essence, they are one. They are intertwined so completely in the creative process that breaking them apart is impossible. In many ways, they're attributes of, and within, each other. They are the defining attributes of the self.

But there's more. And that's why we must continue our journey into the self, not stop here if we intend to live a safe universe. Because it's the fullness of the self that brings the complete understanding we need in order to accept a new definition of the self, and a new working hypothesis on how to approach our dealings with camouflage physical reality. In other words, how to become conscious creators, unburdened with haphazard and unenlightened constructions.

And with that information under our belts, a new dawn will break brighter over our understanding of the self, make no mistake.

A note: Mental acts are highly important to us to understand and ultimately to consciously use, so they will be described in more depth later in this book.

5

Suggestion is no more and no less than an inner willingness and consent to allow a particular action to occur; and this consent is the <u>trigger</u> which sets off the subconscious mechanisms that allow you to construct inner data into physical reality.
—*Seth,* The Early Sessions, Book 2, *Session 68*

Suggestion/Expectation/ Mental Acts

Earlier we learned All That Is continually attempts to materialize some of itself, which it accomplishes, and those attempts result in action. As Seth said then, "Action is the breath of inner vitality (*or All That Is*), of which all materializations of any kind are composed." So, action is the creative force of All That Is, and it is also All That Is expressing itself in different forms and materializations. As Seth reminds us, there is nothing anywhere, ever, that is not All That Is expressing itself as action, and that includes each of us.

And other earlier points to review before we bring in our new topic are that significances define the framework for what individual consciousness can experience in its present state of being; and it is mental acts by consciousness that point toward the significances within its defined range that resonate with those mental acts, the significances which will become materialized under certain conditions.

Now we get to a very intriguing question, one that pinpoints even more precisely the impetus behind creation. What do mental acts intrinsically reflect from within that drives action toward certain creations? A drum roll, please…it is *suggestion*.

Mental acts are suggestion, and as it happens, suggestion is an active part of action. Seth says, "It (*suggestion*) is indeed in the nature of an impetus, an inner impetus that belongs to action, and is not some force separated from action, and acting upon it. … It can even be termed the direction, or the various spontaneous directions, in which action itself moves."[1]

So, suggestion is a characteristic of action, the controlling creative force within it. It's what sets action's course, it's what determines the materializations that action will create, or not create. Suggestion is the powerhouse behind all action in the spacious present, the only place where creation can occur. And it applies to all creations, including Seth's, because suggestion is the bottom line that determines the course of action for *all* consciousness.

Another word for suggestion, according to Seth, is expectation. You cannot pick up a glass of water unless you give yourself the suggestion, however fleetingly, as to your intent, which is actually the expectation that it can happen—indeed, that there is such a thing as a glass, and there is such a thing as water, and even there is such a thing as movement. The couch you sit on would not be in your reality unless you expected/assumed it to be there. When Seth says there are no walls to our house, he's saying they are camouflage found only in our private framework of reality, created or materialized through our mental acts of suggestion/expectation in the spacious present.

So, in creating a chair for his study, Seth has to place *significance* on the kind of chair he desires, and he does it through *suggestion* via his *mental acts*. And that's how we do it too, with every object and event we experience. Seth tells us, "In your system of reality you are learning what mental energy is, and how to use it. You do this by constantly transforming your thoughts and emotions into physical form. You are supposed to get a clear picture of your inner development by perceiving the exterior environment. What seems to be a perception, an objective concrete event independent from you, is instead the materialization of your own inner emotions, energy and mental environment."[2]

Mental Acts

So, suggestions are mental acts that reflect the significance of expectation. But what is expectation in this context? Sure, it means the biggies in experience, such as the expectation we don't need health insurance, or we can find a better job. But it also encompasses the expectation our patio chair will be there when we awake, and there will indeed be a patio. And our muscles will strengthen because we work out, and movement happens in time and space. Whether the suggestion is acceptance of a root assumption agreed to by all, or a new idea we personally come to embrace (such as a flu shot affords protection), suggestions create.

Our realities, then, are created and defined by the expectation within suggestion, and suggestions are mental acts. As we know, mental acts are composed of a combination of the forces of thought, emotion and imagining. Take any other descriptive word for mental act, such as attitude or belief or intent or assumption or—well, you get the idea—and you'll find they all hail back singly or in a combination to these super powerful three basics, the basics that define what we will create.

And since Seth says, "You must understand that each mental act is a reality for which you are responsible,"[3] let's take a brief look at the three components of these mental acts that eventually become suggestions leading to manifestations.

Thought

Seth calls thought an unsurpassable force. He says it is almost as if our thoughts punch the keys of some massive computer, because they do indeed have a force. He also tells us thoughts have a reality and psyche content that has form and shape, and when we finally perceive it, thought has taken on camouflage's bulk. That is, it has become objects and events in our reality. And that is why Seth says, "Your subjective world causes your physical experiences.... See your thoughts as the real events."[4]

Emotion

To get a sense of the dynamic strength of emotion, here's Seth: "Any strong emotion carries within it far more energy than, say, that required to send a rocket to the moon."[5] Emotions bring intensity to our thoughts, which make the combination very powerful.

Think "I am a victim" with emotion behind it, and we all know what happens. But think "I am a victim" as a passing thought, one not dwelled upon or emotionalized, and it grabs little to no creative traction. So, thought and emotion work hand in hand to create expectations, positive or negative.

Imagination

Seth tells us our world and everything in it exists first in the imagination, and imagination is one of the most concentrated forms of energy we possess. So, once more we're introduced to an incredibly powerful force, one, like emotion and thought, that drives creation, one so awesome Seth says that when combined with great expectation, our imagination can materialize almost any reality within the range of probabilities.

And why do these three powerhouses—thought, emotion and imagination—have the heart of creation in their hands? Because they are what form expectations, also known as suggestions. And by now we well know suggestion drives action. So, all of what is created is thanks to suggestion within action. And suggestion is composed of mental acts. And mental acts are composed, to varying degrees and intensities, of thought, emotion and imagination.

And that's why suggestion's mental acts should rivet our attention. Seth says we haven't learned to use our consciousness "properly or fully," because we don't understand that imagination, emotion and thought are not only not set against each other, but are forces joined at the hip, and can be consciously used as such. And if there is one Seth quote that acts as a bridge between the *concept* of mental acts and the all-important *practical using*, it's this one: "You must become consciously aware of what you tell yourself is true every moment of the day, for that is the reality that you project outward."[6] And now we understand why.

Disentangling Negative Suggestions From Action

Are we unequivocally on board with the fact only suggestion/expectation determines the outcome of our individual realities because it is part of action, and all creation is mental? Good, because now we're about to add the final knock-your-socks-off factor to suggestion.

But before we start, while you're reading this section please remember we're talking about consciousness in the spacious present—which is, among all others, *you*. Keep your eyes focused on this truth, as opposed to seeing yourself in linear time. Camouflage linear time is *not* where you reside, so it is not where you solve problems or create goals. And this becomes important in our further steps to redefining the self, so we may as well start remembering it in our *Now*.

Okay, because the spacious present is ordered by significances doesn't mean each consciousness can't create its own intimate, personal chaos. Seth says, "What you term negative suggestions are usually impeding actions, or directions of actions which impede the main directive inner flow. They operate then in much the same manner as crosscurrents, setting up blockages, and impeding main energies by dividing them in several diverse directions."[7]

So, imagine a thick trunk of action, or in ordinary terms let's say it's a goal with expectation behind it. That's our main trunk of action and should, by rights, come into being. But the potential problem? If we give ourselves negative suggestions—not even necessarily having to do with the main goal, but tangential to it—those suggestions cause crosscurrents which divide the main action into several diverse directions, which weaken the main action (our goal) significantly.

Seth continues: "Until the energy, once again, becomes disentangled, action will also flow in the crosscurrents, and the <u>main trunk</u> of energy that gives overall integrity...could, therefore, be severely threatened."[8] Seth again: "It is extremely important that methods be learned to let action follow its normal directive bent within the personality, therefore avoiding these abortive offshoots that impede main directives and purposes of the unit as a whole."[9]

This is a wake-up call for all of us. If we let our negative suggestions build without management, they will impact what we really want out of life, because our main action will not be able to sustain itself.

And Seth finishes with this: "When cross currents of action are constructed, action will continue in those directions unless it is diverted back to other channels. Then the secondary or impeding channel will automatically be closed off. But all action must be withdrawn from it, for as long as the channel remains, then the possibility remains that the impeding action will reoccur."[10]

And if you've ever wondered why you think you've changed a belief and here it comes again, it's because it has shown up in your conscious thoughts or emotions or imaginings as suggestion, maybe in different clothes than originally dressed, but it *had* to be part of your thinking in some form—and the proof is because the channel remained open, or re-opened. No god did it to you, no inner self did it to you, no subconscious did it to you. Nothing trips us up but our own thinking and suggestions.

Awakening From Our Normal Awake State

Everything we've talked about, and will talk about, in this book applies to all consciousness created in the three dilemmas, which is *all consciousness*, ever. None of it is specifically and uniquely directed to consciousness creating camouflage physical reality. That is, creation always happens in the spacious present, it's all started by All That Is, and it's all about significances and action and the suggestions given which direct that action into materializations.

True, entities can and do at times choose to create camouflage frameworks in which it seems action takes place, such as we do with physical reality, but creation outside the spacious present is impossible. Ergo, the camouflage frameworks are meaningful in that they're attempting to structure learning within a given context (think linear time/cause and effect, for instance, or even Seth's framework, whatever it is), but meaningless if it is assumed creation happens within them. It simply cannot, because it's not the way All That Is creates.

The reasons this is so important for us to understand are myriad, but the one to focus on now is that this knowledge helps us to continue to redefine the self. We no longer see our self as caught in linear time/cause and effect, with few creation tools at our disposal we can understand or use. Indeed, we create exactly as Seth or any other identity does, so we're not at a disadvantage of some unknown sort by having chosen physical reality. That's not where our vulnerability lies. If anywhere, it lies in our complete, unchallenged assumption of time being linear, and of the implications of the acceptance of cause and effect. Remember, creation cannot happen in physical reality. It is impossible. It can only look as though it's happening here.

All of this information is so profound in so many ways. One is it sorts out all the misunderstandings of how creation happens, not only misunderstandings by non-metaphysical people, but by those in the New Age too. And along with our sharper knowledge comes a great awareness of how we can practically apply it to our realities and know it will work, because we know how creation works.

But we must come awake first. Seth says, "To understand that you create your own reality requires an 'awakening' from the normal awake state.... This recognition does indeed involve a new performance on the part of your own consciousness, a mental and imaginative leap that gives you control and direction over achievements that you have always performed, though without your conscious awareness."[11]

So, on to the next chapter, folks. It's all about the moment point, and will help us understand how to gain the control and direction Seth mentions that can lead us to living a safe universe.

6

This moment point which appears within your physical universe is but a small materialization of larger portions of the spacious present.

—Seth, The Early Sessions, Book 5, *Session 219*

The Moment Point/Present

As you know, everything being discussed in this book is very specific in its purpose. It is to lead us past the haphazard and unenlightened constructions we seem to stumble into, the ones which reflect an unsafe, not consciously directed, personal reality. And to do that, we seriously need to understand how creation happens. How else can we possibly expect to consciously direct our existence if we don't even have a handle on all aspects of the creative process, not just the few highlighted in pop metaphysical culture?

We're not talking about just consciously creating a goal now and then through focused thought, which many of us have done. We're talking about creating a continuous reality which is safe and trustworthy. Not one without challenges, but one where the challenges aren't driven into existence because of one or more unreasonable fears, or because of a belief in a lack of safety in an inherently uncontrollable reality of cause and effect.

And the only way to do that, according to Seth, is to change our understandings and beliefs about the nature of time. It *always* gets back to time. Living a safe universe consistently and consciously cannot happen without accepting, and then *using*, a uniquely fuller definition of time. And this chapter's subject, the moment point, will catapult us smack into Seth's central premise. You know, the one where linear time/cause and effect is a nonstarter.

The Window of the Present

First, let's take a look at how Seth defines the moment point for himself and his colleagues. He says, "Our work, development and experience all takes place within what I term the 'moment point.' Here, within the moment point, the smallest thought is brought to fruition, the slightest possibility explored, the probabilities thoroughly examined, the least or the most forceful feeling entertained…. The moment point is the framework within which we have our psychological experience."[1]

And Seth explains our moment point in this way: "The moment as you think of it, then, is the creative framework through which you, the nonphysical self, constantly form corporeal reality; and through that window into earthly existence you form both its future and its past."[2] And, "In your terms—the phrase is necessary—the moment point, the present, is the point of interaction between all existences and reality. All probabilities flow through it."[3]

What we're principally dealing with here is the essence of action and its constant thrust forward. The moment point is composed of the amount of action a consciousness is capable of assimilating within its present framework, so our range of action differs from, say, Seth's. Therefore, what we physically see and experience, as we stand at the apex of our moment point, is an ever-changing range of action which fits within linear time's constraints of the moment.

To explain the moment point further, simply to be understood we must use terminology from both linear time and the spacious present, because the moment point straddles our understanding of each reflection of time. So here goes...

What we experience in the current moment point is a by-product of previous mental acts in previous moment points. That experience, that action, is translated by our outer senses into our present moment of camouflage reality. At the same time, we will also direct our next action, one that matches our mental acts of the moment, which could, depending on its intensity, be picked up at another moment point by our outer senses as camouflage reality.

To winnow this down to its importance, think of it this way. The moment point, or present, is the window in which we both a) frame our current mental acts or suggestions which will direct future action; and b) experience the physical materializations of past action, the materializations being our environments, events and bodies.

Actually, more is determined in the moment point. Take the past, for instance. What we give significance to in the present quite literally reorganizes what we think of as our past, thereby constantly changing it. The supposed past is created in the spacious present in the moment point, just as the future is, because the spacious present is the only time there is; and because of action, creation is never stagnant or over.

As Seth tells us, "It should appear obvious from what I am saying that neither future nor past is predetermined. From your platform of poised now-experience, you alter both the past and the future, and that alteration, that change, that action, causes your point of immediate sense life."[4]

So, you might say the moment point is our window of opportunity, if used properly. Actually, you might say the moment point is the only window of opportunity we'll ever get. It's also the window of inopportunity, if used sloppily. Think haphazard and unenlightened constructions, think an unsafe universe.

The Only Time of Significance

Seth uses the moment point somewhat similarly to the way we do, as you'll have noticed in his previous comments. Remember, creation isn't different for consciousness focused in different realities. So, like Seth, we work in the moment point. It's the framework within which we explore our psychological potential. All significances are selected here. All suggestion is applied here. All action happens here. Therefore, all *reality* is created and eventually *met* here.

The unassailable fact is we are personalities which always use the moment point for our immediate focus, and that focus ends up creating our reality. Therefore, the only time of significance in the camouflage of linear time is the moment, the focus point for the mind. And that's why pandering to linear time is self-limiting. Linear time is an hallucinated circumstance, which, when bought into without question or attempts to see <u>and act</u> beyond it, limits our comprehension of ourselves, which limits our experience. As Richard Bach so aptly put it in his book *Illusions*, "Argue for your limitations, and sure enough, they're yours."

Using the Moment Point Wisely

Although you've read them here earlier, both of Seth's following comments fit perfectly with the subject of the moment point, and are an exclamation point way of emphasizing the awesome power of our mental acts and how, when used wisely and well in the present moment, can lead us to living a safe universe. They are also a nice way to end this topic: "You must become consciously aware of what you tell yourself is true every moment of the day, for that is the reality that you project outward." And, "You must understand that each mental act is a reality for which you are responsible."

See you in the next chapter where we'll talk about probabilities and how they play into the moment point, which plays into expanding our notion and definition of the self, which plays into living a safe universe.

7

You are learning how to transform the imaginative realm of probabilities into a more or less specific, physically experienced world.
—*Seth,* The Individual and the Nature of Mass Events, *Session 829*

Probabilities

If anything has become clear through these ongoing discussions, it has got to be the fact that nothing is created in physical reality, all creation happens in the spacious present and then becomes reflected in our camouflage-defined reality. But no creation happens here—not motion, not aging, not growth, because they all depend on time and space being the bedrock requirements of physical creation. But time and space are simply camouflages made possible by the creative abilities of consciousness. They are secondary constructs brought to life because they serve a desired purpose.

And that is precisely why we've not led discussions in this book from a linear time perspective, attempting to understand how to initiate change from within camouflage itself. The dynamics of change simply cannot be understood, let alone deciphered, when viewed as one self moving through one world, on a birth-to-death journey that is basically outside the self's obvious control.

Do you see how our wheels just keep spinning when we bind ourselves to a belief in linear time/cause and effect? How we're then forced to search for answers through psychology and self-help and science and religion—all solidly based on that one belief and, therefore, missing the point entirely? (Much of New Age thinking isn't off the hook, either, in spite of talking a larger picture.)

We simply cannot get from here to there, i.e. living a safe universe, without bringing a heavy dose of reality to our thinking. And this chapter's dose, probabilities, will nudge us even closer to understanding how our true self, honestly and without equivocation, brings about change.

Awash in Probabilities

Seth tells us physical events imply the collection of nonphysical forces into an organization existing outside of time and space. And part of the nonphysical forces he's talking about are probabilities. He says, "Probabilities are an ever-present portion of your invisible psychological environment. You exist in the middle of a probable system of reality. It is not something apart from you. To some extent it is like a sea in which you have your present being. You are in it, and it is in you."[1] "From it you choose those patterns of thought which you will weave into the physical matter of your universe."[2]

So, let's take a look at some of the more intriguing comments Seth makes regarding the nature of the field of probabilities, and we'll get a better sense of what it means to our creation efforts.

"The probable field is strongly composed of thought images, not physically materialized, but extremely vivid and actual storehouses of energy."[3]

Thought images have an amazingly intense energy behind them and an unparalleled role in creation. Even the field of probabilities is composed of thought images (i.e. mental acts, or suggestion). Thought images are action, and action is what directs consciousness through experiences.

"You use probabilities like blocks to build events."[4]

An event can never be created from just one probability, because each probability is an action, with the "next" action terminating the last, flashing on the screen of camouflage reality a whole new scene. An event is actually the result of numerous probabilities linked by significances in the spacious present, based on our mental acts in the moment point—and the *changes* to our mental acts in the moment point, until a certain overall scenario can be said to have been experienced.

As an example, let's say Seth wants to create a whole new study, and he sets it as a goal. That goal is not simply one probability snug and complete, an end product in the field of probabilities. It's a flowing together of many probabilities/actions; or as Seth characterizes it, blocks that build events.

"The nature of any given probable action does not lead to any particular inevitable concluding act."[5]

When Seth set his goal for a new study, he had to have the flexibility of making choices along the way, changing his mind, adding new elements, etc. He started the action with a charged thought, here called a goal, and that one action kicked off the unfolding of other actions which took certain directions as Seth made his choices. But the end result was never an absolute given. For instance, if Seth had let go of his goal for whatever reason, those new thought images would have changed the outcome of his study. So, even though instant materializations of action, one after the other, look to us like an only-one-path-could-have-led-to-it event, there was no one probability encompassed by the totality of Seth's new study, or any given event, for that matter.

"Each event that you form from any given set of probabilities automatically gives rise to new probabilities."[6]

In fact, what Seth chose to eventually experience as his "final" study was itself an arbitrary event, because action doesn't stop still and freeze an event in place. Consciousness can put arbitrary boundaries around an event through focused suggestion, but the event continues to change and expand because of action. And this is what gives us the freedom to open new options in our realities. The options are always there, awaiting our nod of suggestion in whatever direction we wish to go. So, consciousness can expand its event's arbitrary boundaries by growing its suggestions—or by lessening them. Either way, the boundaries are expanded, never contracted, because all change is seen as expansion.

"Before you make your decision, each of these probable actions are equally valid."[7]

Seth could have chosen a blue chair with a matching ottoman

for his study, or he could have chosen to have no chair, but instead a pair of matching couches. The choices were his, via his suggestions and expectation—and each was equally valid, equally available to him, because of the nature of creation, the nature of action. And so are ours, as long as they fall within our framework of significance.

"The main nature of events, the majority of events, do not 'solidify' until the last moment, in your terms."[8]

The field of probabilities assures consciousness it can change its mind at any time and alter the potential outcome of an event. Events can't be decided so far in advance we don't have time to rethink our position. True, there comes a moment when we're committed to the event because our beliefs are so in alignment with it; and true, those beliefs perhaps started the event in the first place. But if we "awake" from the immediate focus on linear time/cause and effect, and instead switch our belief to the one we know to be true about the moment point, suggestion and the spacious present, change can happen.

"At no time are events predestined. At every moment you change, and every action changes every other action."[9]

There can be no predestination, solely because of action's constant forcing of change. We are not, and cannot, be victims to predetermination, by ourselves, our inner selves or some strange energy outside ourselves. Period. If it happens, we created it.

"There are in your terms, then, unlimited probable future events for which you are now setting groundworks. The nature of the thoughts and feelings you originate and those that you habitually or characteristically receive set a pattern."[10]

There's no getting around it—our potential possibilities are the direct result of suggestions, or what we think and feel and imagine in the moment point. Do we want to continually play the past over and over in our mind, looking for reasons for failure or victimization? Or do we want to use the moment point to instead press forward into the future we wish to meet? Either way is up to us, and it's highlighted beautifully in what Seth said earlier: "You must become consciously aware of what you tell yourself is true every moment of the day, for that is the reality that you project outward."

Shifting From Road to Trail

As Seth's lead-in quote to this chapter tells us, we are learning how to transform an imaginative realm of probabilities into a physically experienced world. And he gave Jane and Rob a very thought-provoking example of how changing their suggestions allowed quite a different materialization to happen to what seemed to be their very concrete, finished world. And this one example, more than perhaps anything else we could be told about probabilities, brings them out of theory and into practical daily life.

To set the stage, the year was 1964 and eight months since the first Seth session. Jane and Rob were concerned about what they saw as defects in a small house they'd decided to purchase, but soldiered ahead with an offer. The loan was denied over a technicality. The technicality was the dirt road leading up to the property was appraised as a trail instead of a road, and unless the trail could be maintained by either county or city at no further expense to the Butts family, which it could not, because it was classed as private, the loan was a no go.

In explaining the situation, Seth told Jane and Rob they would have moved in to their new home by the middle of the month, except for one thing. They had physically changed the road to a trail before the appraisal, because they individually and privately had determined they didn't want the property. Their psychic energy, focused on the property, constructed it in their realities with the road disintegrated into a trail. And the reason they could create such a change? Because the material from which all pasts, presents and futures are made is in the field of probabilities.

There's more to this story, and each piece of it fleshes out the picture with more clarity as to how it came about. You can find it in *The Early Sessions, Book 2*, session 79, and it's very much worth the read.

Setting Boundaries of Choice

Even though we see ourselves supposedly in hardcore linear time, our thinking has to transcend linear time. We have to accept ourselves as in the spacious present, surrounded by all possible probabilities; and we have to use suggestion to choose our significances from the field of probabilities. By so doing, we set our boundaries of choice, *by* choice. And then our physical reality will adapt to our changed thinking. We will, quite literally, convert a road to a trail, or vice versa, because the road and trail are simply probable and, therefore, changeable camouflage constructions created in the spacious present by our action, through our expectations.

Seth says, "If you understand the nature of probabilities, you will not need to pretend to ignore your present situation. You will recognize it instead as a probable reality that you have physically materialized. Taking that for granted, you will then begin the process necessary to bring a different probability into physical experience."[11]

And on that note we'll move on to our next chapter where so much more will become clear, especially about the power of our newly defined self.

8

The entity is the basic self, immortal, nonphysical...and has an almost inexhaustible supply of energy at its command. The individual is the portion of the whole self that we manage to express physically...

—*Jane Roberts,* The Seth Material, *Ch. 1*

The Entity and Inner Self

Those of us who have been around the Seth material for any length of time know of the complexity of interrelationships between entities, inner selves, probable selves, dream selves and past, present and future selves, etc., etc. And we know we really cannot separate our "known" self from those other aspects of our overall identity. But if we want to understand today's physical self in a broader framework, we do need to focus down to one relationship that has an immediate, irrevocable, unquestionable impact on us. And that relationship is, of course, to our inner self.

As Seth tells us, "It is only through the recognition of the inner self that the race of man will ever use its potential."[1] That's a very strong statement, and as such should prompt us to seek both knowledge of, and experience with, our inner self, if we at all care about our <u>own</u> potential. So, let's take a look at some of the things

Seth has to say about that part of us that might be termed our inner self.

The Entity—Aka the Soul

But first, in order to understand the inner self, we need a quick refresher on the *entity* for it all to make sense.

Seth says, "There is however a portion of you, the deeper identity who forms both the inner ego (*inner self*) and the outer ego (*physical self*), who decided that you would be a physical being in this place and time. *This* is the core of your identity, the psychic seed from which you sprang, the multidimensional personality of which you are a part."[2] *(A note: Remember from chapter one about identities being formed during the first creative dilemma? Well, entities are part of identities, so that is where they start.)*

Seth expounds on the definition of entity by saying it could be considered a prime identity that is itself a gestalt of many other individual consciousnesses or personalities. And what basically does an entity do? It perceives and creates. And since any act of perception, which is an action, changes reality, an entity is changed constantly because it perceives.

And that is why the entity, or soul, is not static; it grows and develops, as Seth says, through the experiences of those personalities which compose it. It is not a closed system, it is vibrant, alive and loving, constantly seeking growth through its perceptions, and through the perceptions of its personalities.

So, our personal mental and psychic perceptions (which are the *only* kinds of perception, for all consciousness) mean a lot to our entity, because its growth is dependent on *our* growth. And that brings us to the intimacy of assistance we get from our entity, in hopes we will perceive clearly and, one might assume, without creating too many haphazard and unenlightened constructions. And that assistance reaches us through the auspices of our inner self.

Clarifying the Inner Self

The entity makes the decision to "send" part of itself into physical reality as a personality (that's each of us), and assigns another part of itself to create—and constantly re-create—us in our camouflage realities. That portion of the entity Seth calls the inner self. So, while the entity decides part of itself will become physical, it also needs part of itself to oversee the process. And that's our inner self's responsibility.

Seth says our inner self acts as a messenger between the entity and us, the present personality. But it's not just a one-way street, our inner self simply sending us messages. We always have access to our inner self; it is impossible to be cut off from it in any way, because it *is* us, as we are *it*. We're both, first and foremost, simply focuses of our entity.

Seth goes on to tell us our inner self is embarked upon an exciting endeavor of its own, in which it learns how to translate its reality into physical terms *through us*. And, as mentioned, that overseeing includes the actual creation of physical reality. Seth says, "It is the inner self, out of massive knowledge and the unlimited scope of its consciousness, that forms the physical world and provides stimuli to keep the outer ego constantly at the job of awareness. It is the inner self...that organizes, initiates, projects and controls...transforming energy into objects, into matter."[3] And those objects naturally include the camouflage body we inhabit.

So, when Seth tells us we create our own reality, we do, in that we use our mind (which is in the spacious present) to think, feel and imagine its way into suggestions; and then use our brain (which is camouflage in physical reality) to see, feel and imagine probabilities into materialization. But it is the other portion of us, our inner self, that lovingly organizes and controls which creations happen when, and sends the patterns for those creations to our brain for actualization.

Do all mental acts become materialized? Not according to Seth. He says a personality thinks so many thoughts that all of them cannot be turned into camouflage—it would overwhelm the personality. So, a screening process needs to take place, with the most significant thoughts taking precedence, and that screening cannot happen unless it is outside of a time context—which is the spacious present, the working arena of our inner self.

But keep in mind, while the camouflage is prepared by our inner self in the spacious present and presented to our camouflage brain, it's not actually brought into physical existence without us using one of our perceptive mechanisms—sight, touch, hearing, taste or smell—to actualize it. As you'll recall, if we cannot perceive it with one of our senses, it will not materialize. So, it definitely takes both our inner self and each of us to physically manifest our individual realities.

Our Relationship With Our Inner Self

Okay, before we go on with our discussion of the inner self, we need to be really clear we're still talking about the whole; that the inner self and personality are simply the entity doing its thing through different focuses. The creative abilities of the inner self and personality are the creative abilities of the entity (which, don't forget, are the creative abilities of All That Is, as expressed in the three dilemmas).

The point is our inner self <u>is</u> our entity, and <u>we</u> are our entity. And that tells us the overall intent of our entity factors into the purpose of our inner self. And the purpose of our inner self factors into our purpose. We really are one, with our overall intent being uniquely expressed at different flash points of reality for each of us as lines of development. As Seth says, "You <u>are</u> your soul."

So, what is our relationship with our inner self, once we choose physical life? It's rather obvious we're never separated from it. How could we be? It's what we're made of, which makes separation impossible. But that is not to say our inner self takes over our decisions for us, just because we are so tightly connected. It has its own way of approaching its purpose, and is given great leeway by the entity to do so. And we are afforded the same opportunity. However, if we stray too far from the general line of development we agreed to pre-birth, all hell breaks loose.

Perhaps "hell" can be defined as the haphazard and unenlightened constructions Seth talks about. Certainly it's a wake up call. Seth says, "The ego that ignores too many of the possibilities of the inner self is soon in dire difficulty, and is forced to realize that it has been considering survival in a very limited light."[4]

The overall goal between our inner self and us seems to be expansion of consciousness, also called growth or value fulfillment by Seth. And he clarifies it with this: "In true expansion of consciousness, you become more and more aware, more <u>conscious</u> of inner realities that were previously never realized on a conscious level. ... (The ego) recognizes its identity <u>as part of</u> the inner self. ... In other words, portions of the inner self have joined the strictly egotistical functions. The ego in such cases is so attuned that it becomes almost something else."[5]

Given our inner self has such high stakes riding on us, does it step in and control our thoughts, emotions and imaginings to its advantage, since those mental acts signal the direction of creation? Unfortunately for us, no. As Seth tells us, we are on our own, "with the power of self-determination and free will." And he adds that no commands are built-in, no prohibitions given; it is each of us who make our own choices.

The Gift of Backup

Ah, but thankfully for us our inner self has our back. While it won't step in and force a decision change, it will do its best to point us in a more constructive direction. In fact, that is our inner self's overall responsibility, part of its *raison d'être*.

For instance, Seth tells us when our inner self is alerted to a problem, it will immediately try to remedy the situation by an influx of self-corrective measures which, hopefully, we will accept and run with. And going even further with its assistance, Seth says occasionally when a problematic situation gets out of hand, our inner self will bypass the more constrained areas of our conscious mind, and try to solve the problem by sending energy into other layers of activity. But note the words *try* and *gets out of hand* in the last sentences. And then think about what they mean to your situation under advisement and your approach to handling it. Time to take a deep, steadying breath?

One comment of Seth's, which seems to draw the attention of his readers almost with a sigh of relief, is when he says the inner self "will sift from the barrage of conflicting beliefs the particular set that is the most life-giving," and send these in what then appears as a revelation. And he says such revelations result in new patterns that can change behavior. Another time Seth tells us it is of significant value to remember this inner affiliation, because such an affirmation of belief can often allow our inner self to send needed messages of love, strength or balance, appearing as inspiration, perhaps bursts of feeling or dreams; and even as thoughts, images and impulses.

And when we listen or react positively to the offered assistance, the merging of intent by our inner self and us is at its equinox. We're then sharing the same path toward value fulfillment, we're headed in the same direction. As Seth reminds us, "The personality itself is a gestalt of action, and as such it is necessary that the flow of action within it follow the overall directives of the entity and inner self."[6]

But to believe we can "let go, let God," or assume our inner self is watching our back on all decisions and choices to the point where it will safely guide us through life simply out of its love for us, is a complete misunderstanding of the role of the inner self, and ours too. It is not a god to be surrendered to. It is our <u>partner</u> in the creation process.

I'm of the mind one of the biggest stumbling blocks to complete acceptance of responsibility for our life is because of a distorted or unclear belief about the role of our inner self. And it isn't a small thing. It muddies our mind so we're never sure who's creating what, and for what reason; or who's doing what to whom, and why. We need to get clear with ourselves on this very intricate and important point, if we have any hope of living a safe universe.

A New Definition of Strength

The whole point of this book is to expand our understanding of the self so we can use more of our creative abilities consciously. And there is zero way our self can be understood without taking into consideration our inner self. Seth makes this abundantly clear in this comment, if strength is equated to living fulfilling realities: "True strength is the result of excellent communication between the outer self that faces the world, and the inner self that looks inward."[7]

So, how do we align our known self with our inner self? There's really only one way, and it's through trust. Which just happens to be the upcoming discussion.

Many of you keep searching for some seemingly remote spiritual inner self that you can trust and look to for help and support, but all the while you distrust the familiar self with which you have such intimate contact.
—*Seth,* The Individual and the Nature of Mass Events, *Session 872*

Trust

Seth tells us we have the power to change our lives and the world for the better. And in his books we're told how to do it. We're not given esoteric instructions that skim the surface of physical reality, teaching us how to handle our suffering, not how to transcend it. And we're not told to pray to the gods of our current civilization to bail us out of our troubles, hoping like crazy they know what they're doing, since it's obvious we don't.

No, we're told *we* have the power to change our lives and the world for the better—no strings attached. And thanks to Jane and Rob's enormous contribution to humanity, we know how to do it. We Seth readers have some of the clearest information available in today's world at our fingertips. It gives us the most concise description of man's interaction with the universe found in literature available today. And because of it, we know freedom, the greatest freedom available to humankind—because we know we create our realities, and by knowing it, we can learn to change what we don't like.

We've come a long way in our personal understandings, and the focus of this book has been on broadening the definition of the self so we can live a safe universe. That's our goal, and good for us, we've learned or remembered many of Seth's concepts which dovetail with our need for that expanded learning. But as we know quite well, knowledge itself will not set us free. If that were the case, we'd all be healthy, wealthy and wise after reading our first Seth/Jane book.

What does it take, then, to make the leap from pure knowledge-based concepts we fully accept as valid, to actually translating that knowledge into living a safe universe? This is no big secret, we all know the answer: a blending of knowledge and trust. Trust takes us beyond accepted knowledge, into a mental and imaginative awakening that allows conscious direction to guide our creations. Without trust, we cannot take the necessary and fulfilling step of *living* the results of our learning.

So, what is it we have to trust? How about our literal oneness with All That Is and our inner self? The simultaneous and subjective nature of time, ergo the lack of cause and effect? That what we see is actually camouflage in the spacious present dressed to look as though it resides in time and space? That action, the driving force of creation, is given direction through suggestion composed of thought, emotion and imagination? Okay, the list goes on and on, no doubt about it. So much to learn to trust, it seems.

But is that true? Is there really so much to trust? In one regard yes, because each of those components of knowledge, and many others, are actually facts we must accept as true if we're to throw off the yoke of the one-line stage of consciousness Seth discusses, and stop creating haphazard and unenlightened constructions. So they can't be downplayed. But they *can* be gathered under the banner of a whole trust, one trust that, by nature, encompasses—nay, transcends—the sum of its parts. And that one trust is of our self.

Learning to Trust

Seth tells us, "In each person, the ultimate and unassailable and unquenchable power of All That Is is individualized, and dwells in time."[1] And he says, "There is a portion of All That Is directed and focused within each individual, residing within each consciousness. Each consciousness is, therefore, cherished and individually protected."[2] This, then, is the ultimate basis for our trust, the platform upon which we stand, and which never wavers or changes. It simply is.

But that's not always clear to those of us consciousness in physical reality. We've lost the sense of being a part of All That Is. Seth says it's critically important we get the feeling back, though. He also says All That Is needs to be experienced in order to be comprehended. So, I asked myself on my quest for trust, how does one experience All That Is? My seeking led me back to one of my favorite Jane Roberts books, *The Afterdeath Journal of an American Philosopher: The World View of William James*. James makes All That Is come alive in our imaginations, in our thinking, in our hearts. Some have called it the most brilliant description of All That Is ever penned, and I agree.

In *Afterdeath Journal*, James describes his subjective environment after his death, and the feel of All That Is within that environment. Here's some of what he says about his experience with All That Is, taken from Chapter 10: The Atmospheric Presence.

"Everywhere I sense a presence, or atmosphere, or atmospheric presence that is well-intentioned, gentle yet powerful, and all-knowing. ... At the risk of understating, this presence seems more like a loving condition that permeates existence, and from which all existence springs. The feeling of safety is definitely connected here, in that I know that no evil or harm can befall me, that each of my choices will yield benefits, and that this loving condition upholds me in all of my ways. ... I *know* that this presence or loving condition forms itself into me, and into all other personalities; that it lends itself actively to seek my good in the most particular and individual ways."

And in Chapter 11: The Divine Mood, James continues: "The words 'psychological growing medium' come to mind, as if this atmosphere promotes psychic growth to the most advantageous degree.... This good intent is seemingly directed toward me because I am me; and I sense a deep understanding on its part of my subjective reality.... It quietly offers—what? Solace, support, a buoyancy in which my existence is everywhere strengthened, refreshed.... I do know that this same atmospheric presence and knowing light also sustains earth."

James' Perspective on Faith

That's what William James knows. He doesn't have to take it on faith, because he so closely experiences All That Is within his afterdeath environment. But as physical consciousness, we chose to separate ourselves from our inner knowledge in order to experience certain growth, so we don't seem to have the sensory clarity of All That Is that James does. But now, Seth says, the time for such feelings of separation must come to an end. It's time to move on.

To integrate complete trust into our lives, it helps to see faith's principles from James's perspective. Here's some of what he says on this subject in Chapter 13: Biological Faith and Nature's Source: "To the extent that faith applies to anything, then it is trust in one's natural order of being; the feeling that conditions are largely conducive to it; that needs will be met within the circumstance of that natural order; and that one is couched and supported in one's existence by some larger Nature from which the natural order springs. ... Faith I now see is a more general omnipresent quality that is best not attached to any particulars."

That's where we're trying to go in our psyches, into a faith so much a part of the fabric of our being, so much a part of our belief in ourselves as a portion of All That Is, that trust itself becomes commonplace to us. We want to be where James was when he made this comment: "So natural do I now find this faith that it is hard to believe it was not a conscious part of my mental constitution during life."[3]

Coming to Trust Our Self

But, at times, maybe most times at first, we can't see it, so we attempt to answer the questions of the mind in order to allow ourselves to trust. That's what drew many of us to the Seth material in the first place, this need for answers, perhaps even when we weren't aware that was our cause or path. So, answering the questions is important, because the self's inner desire is to trust; and the mind, in order to trust, normally needs understanding and assurances.

As we develop our understanding of the Seth material and experience it in our daily lives, change starts showing itself here and there, because we start to trust here and there. But what we ultimately need is full, unilateral trust. And Seth tells us, "That trust is within you whether or not you recognize it, for it gives you your present experience; and no matter how your mind questions, it resides securely in the great creativity of the soul."[4]

So, what is it we need to trust, in more concrete terms? According to Seth, "You must trust the self that you <u>are</u>, now."[5] He adds that we must trust our own nature, for it has a purpose. And, "What is needed is a basic trust in the nature of vitality, and faith that all elements of experience are used for a greater good."[6] He says more than that, of course, but those quotes seem to cover the basics.

Do we have any wiggle room with a full commitment to trust in our self, perhaps just trusting sometime? Ha! Our friend and advisor says, "You cannot equivocate: you trust the self or you do not."[7] And one of my favorites, because it so sounds like Seth and makes me smile each time I read it, "You must begin to trust your self some time. I suggest you do it now."[8]

So, yes, it is the self which must come to be trusted, not in selected instances, but always. When we create an event, uneasy or not, we must trust there is purpose and meaning behind it. When we ask for understanding and clarity, we must trust it will always be forthcoming. When we feel an impulse, we must trust there is good intent driving it. When we need healing, psychic or physical, we must trust we are fully capable of creating a path that fits our needs. When we seek new direction, we must trust probabilities to open that guide us.

In other words, we must accept a new, broader definition of our self—and trust it. This book is dedicated to helping build that trust.

10

I am saying that the individual self must become consciously aware of far more reality; that it must allow its recognition of identity to expand so that it includes previously unconscious knowledge. To do this you must understand that man must move beyond the concepts of one god, one self, one body, one world, as these are currently understood.

—*Seth,* The "Unknown" Reality, Vol. One, *Session 687*

A New Definition of Self

So, there you have it, the unique pieces of the Seth material I finally came to see as a whole, the whole that changed my life: All That Is, action, the spacious present, significances, suggestion/mental acts, the moment point, probabilities, entity and inner self, trust. These subjects are now one in my mind, one life-giving, life-changing whole. By now they're so much a part of my thinking, I almost cannot remember how or why I bought so heavily into linear time and the cause and effect that goes with it. These pieces brought me to the understanding, and then the belief, that I could live a safe universe. Not one without challenges, but one based on knowledge and trust.

And why might this be true, that these pieces could lead to living a safe universe? First, because all of them combined are already an integral part of the self. They simply have not been recognized for their importance to the self or its creation efforts; yet not one of them can be eliminated without making a self <u>impossible</u>. And since each one is a part of the self, their built-in conditions of creation, or propensities toward creation, are accessible to the self. Of course, they always were, but now, seen as self, they can be consciously used and directed.

Take action, for instance. We now know we are action, and action is the force behind creation. We also know our mental acts are action, and when they reach the strength of expectation/suggestion, they create events and material objects. And we know action can get entangled in its own negativity, and until the entanglement is straightened out, action will continue along the same lines. So, do you see how knowing how action works can be to our great advantage, if we choose to implement that knowledge? And so it goes with each portion of the self.

So, what is this new definition of our self, then? Here's a quick version, to be fleshed out later in the book with examples, comments, stories and tips. But even this version is only words on paper until the magic of it permeates our thinking, until our hearts beat faster at its recognition. To help the magic along, I'll use words up-close and personal for each of us, in describing this most magical of subjects, our self.

My Self Redefined

I am part of All That Is, from whom I can never be separated. Because I am part of All That Is, I share its creative abilities and processes. They are gifts of my nature.

I am action, the inner vitality of All That Is, and am conscious of myself. My consciousness is a focus through which I experience myself, and "myself," in complete terms, includes my entity, inner self and focus personality. I am always all of these, because they cannot be separated.

I am a part of the spacious present. I cannot be removed from it, because it is within All That Is, as is everything. One of my gifts is my ability to *pretend* to leave the spacious present, and I do this for my own growth and expansion, or value fulfillment.

I define my self through my significance, by what I consider significant for my chosen focus or line of development. My significance is my boundary. It is inviolate; it cannot be breached by another consciousness. I am completely safe within my significance.

I psychologically explore my significance through my mental acts, which act as gateways to new experiences within my significance. My moment point is my point of action within my significance.

I am in constant communication with my inner self. With its help, I simultaneously create and experience in my moment point a present, a remembered past, and the outline of a future, all called into being by probabilities addressed by my mental acts. My inner self depends on me to furnish the clear mind that allows this to occur, without psychological complications that alter our preferred line of development for me.

What my inner self needs of me is trust. Trust is what I am learning in my chosen field of significance. And the more I choose trust over doubt and fear, the more my inner self and I grow into our potential. At that point, we are unstoppable.

Implications and Further Clarifications

If we truly believe everything herein, we will have redefined our self. We will have fully accepted the fact we are not primarily a human in linear time, but instead a consciousness in the spacious present, simply using the camouflage of linear time/cause and effect and matter for our own purposes. And from that point of reference, we will finally be able to bring far more conscious choice and direction to our reality.

And, thankfully, we will not have to remember this new definition word for word. What's important, though, is that we get the sense of it, the feel of it—and accept it. And then when we get to the next chapter, we'll see how to translate our understanding and acceptance into practical experience—and that's what really counts.

As a way of helping with that understanding and acceptance, below is a bulleted list of what we've discussed in the previous chapters. It does not include all points mentioned, but main ones that give the overview of how consciousness, physical and otherwise, creates. Its purpose: We need to know, clearly and without equivocation, that we create *just as any consciousness does*.

So, here we go, then, a cheat sheet of reminders for daily contemplation, starting at the "top" and working "down:"

* Nothing exists but the spacious present, which is within All That Is.

* Consciousness never leaves the spacious present.

* Simultaneous time in the spacious present is the only time there is. All other time is camouflage.

* All action (creation) can <u>only</u> happen within the spacious present, and each action terminates the previous action.

* Each action is a probability. It takes many probabilities to create an event.

* Because of action's constant terminations of the previous action, there can be no *objective* continuity, such as continuous matter or pasts, presents and futures.

* There is, however, a *subjective* continuity, created through the mental expectations and suggestions of consciousness in the moment point.

* All consciousness creates frameworks for experience within the spacious present. Ours is the framework of a physical reality, and it is created by our inner self under the auspices of our entity, with

the root assumptions of time, space and matter.

* My framework for experience is within my dimension of existence, and no other consciousness can breach it.

* Through telepathy, agreement is reached between us personalities that defines what we wish to jointly experience. For a room, for instance, we agree on its furniture, colors, etc. Then the room is created in our individual realities within our individual dimensions of existence.

* Our individual camouflage physical reality blinks off and on millions of times a second, terminating and then re-creating itself constantly.

* Our mind exists in the spacious present. Its mental acts, or suggestion/expectation, in the moment point directs action and, therefore, probabilities, creating our current present, remembered past and outlined future simultaneously in the Now, through this *subjective continuity*.

And that is why everything that happens in our camouflage realities, in what we perceive as linear time, is AFTER THE FACT, why there is no CAUSE AND EFFECT in a physical reality.

Events as a Portion of Our Self

Since we create our own realities, and events are part of our realities, events are literally a translation of a portion of our psyche into a physical manifestation. In other words, they are a part of our self, not separated from us. As Seth says, we translate what we are into an event we can understand.

So, what precisely does that mean to us? Basically, it means we cannot view physical reality and assess its supposed facts for understanding, because what we're seeing is camouflaged psychological actions, not acts caused by some event that came before it. And that's why attempting to solve problems based on our exposure to linear time events is, well, dumb. The answers do not, and cannot, reside in the exterior of linear time events. They can only reside solely in the thinking, the feeling, and the riffs of imagination which brought the exterior events into being, the ones we play out in the spacious present, through our moment points.

Take our environment. However it is built, whatever its condition, it is a direct translation into camouflage of what happens first in the spacious present. Sure, a broken-down car is a physical object. But it starts life as a mental act, or series of mental acts, in the spacious present. Not that we mentally project a broken-down car per se. But did we hold a weary belief about life? A belief about how striving never really works for us, just take a look at the old junker we drive? Or love of old craftsmanship? A reminder of a beloved father? Happiness because we were able to buy it, our first car? Only we can figure out our own physical symbols, but rest assured they started life not objectively, but subjectively.

And since we're taking responsibility for everything in our reality, let's flash to our childhood for a moment. Good for us if we created the perfect family life to be born into. Bad for us if we didn't? Absolutely not. Our pre-birth choices in the spacious present were purposely made to direct our growth/value fulfillment along certain lines. No matter the conditions we found ourselves in, we set it all up. And there are no exceptions to this.

So, instead of bemoaning our childhood or any other "past" event, it's far more productive to take responsibility and figure out why we chose those conditions, what we learned from them, and how to use that knowledge to flesh out our life in a new fashion. And we can even terminate a lot of limiting beliefs about the people involved when *we* take responsibility for *their* participation in our lives.

Events as Integral to Our Self

Here's an interesting example of thought and emotions (i.e. subjective mental acts) becoming a physical object. My daughter and son-in-law had been trying to get pregnant with their first baby for many years, including several attempts with in vitro fertilization. At one point, they hit the depths of despair after hearing the latest in vitro didn't take. They arrived home from the doctor's office feeling broken and sad. As they pulled into their driveway, a partially deflated balloon a couple feet off the ground, dragging its dirty string, floated by their garage door. On it were the words, "Welcome home, Baby."

Here's another example, only this one is about how thought and emotions (i.e. subjective mental acts) create an objectified physical event. It was 1984, and I'd been reading the Seth material for maybe five months. I'd become interested in the Edgar Cayce material also, as I felt my way through my first introduction to all things metaphysical. The Cayce A.R.E. headquarters is in Virginia

Beach, Virginia, and while I strongly wanted to visit it, I couldn't find time to fly from California to Virginia. I was a product manager with Apple at the time, and within weeks of forming that visitation goal, I found myself in Boston on business. It was a Friday, and I was to head home the next day. Instead, my boss phoned and asked if I'd fly to Norfolk, Virginia for the weekend and take care of some business there on Monday.

And it struck me like a thunderbolt—Virginia Beach is only about twenty miles from Norfolk, and I'd have the whole weekend free. I froze in place; I even recall exactly what I was wearing. That was my first experience of consciously *knowing* what had actually happened in the spacious present; that is, what caused the shift in plans.

And years later, after many such events had been noticed by me, this one still sticks in my mind. Stan and I lived with many cats over the years, and among them was a kitten we'd nursed since birth. Pierre was born with a nasty eye condition, and because of it spent considerable time at the veterinarian's during his first four months of life. No surprise if you knew Pierre, he ended up stealing the office staff's collective heart. Eventually we moved Pierre and his siblings to another vet. Seven years went by. One day I was sitting alone in the living room, reminiscing about Pierre's baby days and smiling at memories of his many loveable antics in the first vet's office. The phone rang, and a woman introduced herself as the receptionist from that first office. She said she was calling to remind Lynda of her cat's appointment the next day. After some confusion, the issue was resolved: She had dialed the wrong number, looking for a different Lynda.

Multifaceted Events

But perhaps the story that best captures the multifaceted nature of events comes from this one about Kelly. Or, more accurately, from my torn and shattered psyche after Stan died, and my definite need to know my inner self was more than a mere concept, that it deeply cared for me and had my back. I needed to feel trust.

For background, Stan and I lived in Eugene, Oregon, and we had a cabin on a Washington island in the Columbia River, four hours from Eugene. The island, heavily into dairy life, was well populated with cats, and about 20 or so decided to call our property home. Stan and I, either alone or together, traveled between Eugene and the island regularly, but there were times when we'd be absent for many days. So, we set up an elaborate long-term feeding system for our cats, resupplied by a local lad when needed. And because of the inclement weather the area was noted for, we provided a three-car pole garage with bedding on shelves that allowed them privacy and security.

Kelly was one of the wild ones, beautiful in her long-haired calico colors, petite, exuberant in her play. Kelly ran with the wind, raised her face to the sun, tumbled in the river grass. An outdoors girl born and bred, and not needing or desiring human intervention in her life other than food, thank you very much.

It was shortly after Stan's passing, and I didn't think I could handle another thing. Exhausted and infinitely sad, I went to the island to take care of the cats, and to try to get my first full night's sleep in two weeks. I arrived just before dusk, the cool spring air balm for my bruised spirit. While the large cat feeders never lacked dry food, it had always been our pleasure to dole out canned food immediately upon arrival. So, I set about the task, scratching heads as I plied the deck with plates of food. I was surprised to see Kelly nearby the group; it was her habit to wait further out on the sand for her dish, in case we'd try to kidnap her into the house, or something. I set a plate for her way to the side, where she would feel safe.

After dinner I was cleaning up the debris when I noticed a wet stain on the deck, about six inches in diameter. I touched my finger to it, raised it to my nose, and smelled something rotten. God-awful rotten. And then I saw Kelly, still on the deck next to her untouched plate, watching me, another stain spreading around her back paws. For the first time since I'd arrived, I stepped outside my own misery and noticed it in Kelly. She looked sunken, her fur dull, her body listless. Clearly, something bad was happening to her.

In her one year of life, Kelly had never been within ten feet of Stan or me. Despair grabbed my heart. *I can't help you, baby. I haven't a clue how to help you.* I went inside the house and cried. I cried for myself, my helplessness, for Kelly and her helplessness. Then I started asking my inner self for guidance, for assistance, for *caring*, dammit.

Through a large window, I saw Kelly walk slowly and halt-ingly toward a tree, where, like a worn old tabby in pain, she curled up on the soft soil underneath it. To die? Surely. And that's what pulled me out of my spiritual and mental lethargy, the thought that Kelly was dying and I wasn't doing a damn thing about it.

It was going to take a miracle, but hey, I supposedly believe in them. In the garage, I pulled down one of the cat carriers and walked toward Kelly's tree. About eight feet away, I slowly dropped to the grass and talked soothingly to her. Then I started inching my way closer and closer, very cautiously pushing the carrier ahead a little at a time. Kelly was watchful, but didn't move. Finally the carrier was within two feet of her, the door open wide and a towel on its floor. I sat patiently and waited, talking softly at times, at other times remaining silent. To my joy, Kelly finally heaved herself upright and moved toward the carrier. This kitty who had never been in a carrier, who had never been so physically close to a human, crawled in and laid down. I had my miracle.

And then I blew it.

There was still the door to close. With racing heart and damp hands, I reached too quickly for the door and tried to slam it shut before Kelly could react. But wild cats are quicker than greased lightening, even when terribly ill. Kelly was free of the carrier in a split second, running and then dragging herself into her beloved, protective bramble bushes.

Miserable and shaking, I reentered the house and again cried. But before I could sink into complete despair, the fact Kelly and I had created a miracle between us sprang into awareness in my heart. Could we do it again?

I sat the carrier on the deck, this time where I could see it from the front door, propped it open with a small rock, fluffed the towel, put food and water close by, and waited. Some other cats came to check it out, but none entered its interior. Finally, as the moon rose high in the inky sky, Kelly crawled out of the brambles and made her way to the carrier. She slept inside that night, for the first time in her young life. I didn't sleep at all. I kept watch on Kelly.

At 6:00 that morning, I called the island vet and told her the story. I said I'd be bringing Kelly to the office soon, if she didn't bolt again. With hammering heart, I once more approached the carrier. Only this time when I talked to Kelly, I told her it was up to her, I couldn't help her unless she wanted my help, I'd do anything in the world for her, but she had to trust me, she had to stay in the carrier, no matter what. Then, with trembling hand, I slowly, very slowly, slid the rock from its holding place and reached for the carrier door. Kelly didn't move a muscle, her eyes never left mine. With great caution, I closed the door. She still didn't move, not until I picked up the carrier—and then all hell broke loose.

Kelly went wild, bouncing around the carrier's inside as though she was healthy or something. I beamed. I smiled. I talked soothingly. I hurried to the veterinarian's office. There we found Kelly's uterus was rotting. At first the doctor said she wouldn't operate for 24 hours, giving Kelly enough antibiotics to strengthen her chances during surgery. But an hour later, she called to say Kelly was sinking fast, and the operation had to happen immediately.

A week later, I brought Kelly home to her sand and sun. The first thing she did was head for the water, stand at its edge with her tail in the air, back stretched, and head up. And she never came within ten feet of me again, nor did she ever sleep in the carrier.

Kelly's Event Explained

Trust. It was about learning trust. And it was more than that too. It was an event created through my emotions about the ending of our life on the island as we'd known it. It was about Stan and his great love of our cats, and my sorrow at seeing them without him in this reality. And it was my feeling of helplessness in trying to sort out what to do about our cabin, and knowing I'd soon be faced with the heartbreaking and almost overwhelming job of finding each of our cats a good home.

Seth says we cannot separate our self out of any event we experience, because we are in it, and it is in us. We are, quite literally, what we experience, both inside and out. And for what makes this uniquely true, I remind you of what I wrote in chapter three: "So, realities exist within the identity/action's dimension of existence, not alone or separate from the identity, shuffled off somewhere outside of it. And the ego consciousness (personality), being a portion of the identity, isn't plopped down *outside of its reality* and told to go create. Since realities are a *part* of identity/action, they cannot be separated from an identity, and nothing in a reality can be called not-self, because the self is the *whole* of the action."

We are consciousness. We create. And we're here to learn just exactly what that means. So, on to the next chapter where we'll take a good look at what we can do by choice to set our consciousness in play, in order to live a safe universe.

There simply is no time as you think of it, only a present in which all things occur.
—*Seth,* The Nature of Personal Reality, *Session 669*

Learning to Trust the Moment Point

As Seth tells us, "Continuity, therefore, is in terms of the self rather than in terms of a series of moments. <u>Instead there is a series of selves.</u>"[1] What we are creating in each moment point with each action is a different version of our self. So, in essence, we are learning to create our self by using the energy of which we are already a part. You could say we're learning to handle the inexhaustible energy of the self that is available to us.

And along with this learning comes responsibility, the responsibility to recognize and use the ways in which our emotional, mental and psychic existence creates both form and events, moment by moment. And to what avail? Seth: "To the extent that you understand and utilize the various aspects of consciousness, you will learn to understand your own reality, and the conscious self will truly become conscious."[2] Once we intellectually understand the nature of reality and the self, it only makes sense we can then learn to manipulate within that environment to some extent, because we know more of what we're dealing with.

A long learning process kicked off for me when I set my sights on learning how to live a safe universe. It actually took years to see the picture I eventually became comfortable with, the picture outlined in this book. To me, it is the most logical understanding I could reach that outlined the aspects of creation that concerned me. But it wasn't only cobbling together certain knowledge that brought me to trust—ah, if only that were the case. The biggest challenge, it turned out, was using what I was learning. And the big lesson of what I was learning was that there is no cause and effect, or creation, in linear terms; but that the moment point is the point of creation. That meant I had to reorient my thinking to the moment point, and start *using* the moment point as my pallet of creation.

Clearly, there's no way to pass on to you a path, a simple step-by-step procedure that leads to trust. Trust is too personal, too subjective, too tied to each of our private moments of reality to offer a one-size-fits-all program. I'll gladly share some of the things I learned along the way and some of the tools I developed for my own use, but they may or may not resonate with how you subjectively get hold of an idea and run with it. Trust has to grow in each of our hearts and souls at our own pace and in a form we will accept, based on who and where we are, as consciousness in physical form. But, ultimately, it is *trust in the moment point* that will determine our ability to live a safe universe.

This chapter, then, is a potpourri of advice, results, reflections, suggestions, anecdotes and Seth comments, spontaneously offered to your spontaneous self. It's meant as a place for ideas that may spur new ways of thinking, or perhaps deepen acceptance of things long known. Either way, everything in it is aimed at learning to trust the moment point. So, what I offer here is in the spirit of sharing, knowing it may not resonate with you. And that's just fine. Some day perhaps we will meet and you can fill me in on what you found for yourself, and we just may be amazed at how differently our paths to trust unfolded—or how similarly.

My Personal Kick-Off

I write this book from a personal position of safety and trust. Not that all events I meet are hunky-dory, not at all; but I far better understand their purpose in my life now. So, I view them and their present outcome through a prism of safety and trust. That is, the events themselves may seem at first glance to be off-kilter, but only if I fall into cause and effect thinking. If I stay in the framework of the moment point, where time is simultaneous and I know I create from my center outward, or get back to it quickly, things click back into perspective. I remember I am the cause of the event, that every event serves a purpose, and the purpose is intimately tied directly to me.

I also trust there is a workable solution to the off-kilter event, perhaps not yet known consciously by me, but there nonetheless; and once I'm clear, I'll see or understand it. And the workable solution can run the gamut from an aha moment that immediately changes everything, to simply letting the present outcome go, with trust that I will mentally bounce back in my next moment point, perhaps even opening new paths not previously seen. What the workable solution never is, however, is a Hail Mary pass, hoping like the devil things will work out just because my inner self loves me. The solution's basis is in remembering that I <u>am</u> my inner self, and therefore solutions are naturally there for me, moment by moment.

You see, safety really is all about trust. Without trust in our self, we cannot live a safe universe. It's that simple. That is why, as I mentioned in the Introduction, finding trust became my task after Stan's passing and the events I created. And I soon found I needed to fully reorient my thinking, because as strongly as I wanted to consistently feel trust, my old way of thinking overrode it most of the time. It then became apparent I had to teach myself to think differently. Not the process of how thoughts enter my mind, but the selection and makeup of thoughts themselves in the moment point.

That was all in retrospect, though. In the beginning, I honestly had no idea where to start to find trust. I'd spent years thinking personal beliefs were the answer; that is, find ones that were not in alignment with what I wanted out of life and change them, and that would do the trick. But it did not. It straightened out some things for me at times, but it never brought me that complete understanding, that complete trust, that underlying safety I sought.

How could it? My thinking was still predicated on an overriding belief in linear time/cause and effect, which meant I still laid out my *thinking* in past, present and future format. In other words, I had an intellectual belief in simultaneous time, but I treated my thoughts as though linear time/cause and effect was real, along with its consequences.

And its consequences hammered me at times. Worse, they reinforced the idea of separation. I could claim to understand I wasn't separate from my inner self, but because of what I faced at times when I thought I was doing everything right, doubts about my ability to consciously set a direction of choice flared much too often. And well they should have, because *I did not know how to make it work*. But it wasn't my ability that was lacking, it was my knowledge that could lead to trust.

Separation. It all felt like separation to me, even though I knew that not to be the case. So, the first thing I decided to do, way back when, was to get a grip on a feeling of oneness with All That Is, a living, spiritual connection that would permeate my moments—well, a good portion of them, anyway. In the chapter on trust, I talked about William James and his afterdeath sense of what he called the atmospheric presence and divine mood, and that turned out to be my starting point. I read James' words, and re-read them, and read them again and again. I took notes, I broke James' comments down into simple one-line sentences and created a document I could take on long contemplative walks. I read the document during focused quiet times at home and in the car on extended drives.

What led me to do this was a reflection of how taken I was with the atmosphere or mood of the afterdeath environment. It sounded so supportive and loving, gentle yet powerful, so truly tuned to each of us in its superlative intent to help. And from what James said and my own intuition, I felt I could experience that same mood or atmosphere right here, right now, if only I allowed it. If only…

Then what I consider a breakthrough moment happened. I was starting to get a sense of the atmospheric presence surrounding me, but it wasn't without focused effort, such as in psy-time or meditation. What I needed was one line that would bring the feeling close to me simply upon my thinking it, something that would encompass an immediate sense of the afterdeath divine mood felt by William James, something I could translate into my moment points that would ground me when I dwelled on it any time day or night. Something that tied together the afterdeath condition and my current focus outward into my physical reality.

I found the line and it became a touchstone of great import to me, and to this day is alive and well in my thoughts and emotions. The line of James' is: "A steady confidence sustains me, and a stronger sense of balance than I have ever known." That line embodies what James feels after death when surrounded by the sensation of All That Is. It allows him to settle in and become what the atmosphere promotes. And knowing that, and that James says the same atmospheric presence surrounds us in physical life too, the line became my touchstone as well as my goal. It was what I had always craved in life, a steady confidence grounded in my feeling of closeness with All That Is, one that would bring me a strong sense of balance within my self, within my moments. And I craved it not only for the feelings I wanted to experience, but because I know that thoughts and feelings *create*. What better mindset, then, as I go about creating my reality, than one of strength and balance?

Almost everything I now do with the Seth material has its purpose in that quote. It has become, for me, the embodiment of my own purpose for this lifetime. I see it as the ultimate possibility

found in physical reality, the perfect platform upon which to consciously stand, the platform defined by trust of self. And the only
one for me upon which to build a sustainable personal safe universe.

I highlight my one line here, because when I went back into the
Seth material to find what I had missed for so many years, I was
specifically focused on finding the knowledge that tied the creation
aspects all together for me. I needed to see the logic, the building
blocks, the clarity behind creation so I had a path to believe in and
follow. I simply do not do well with loosey-goosey. And my one
line gave me purpose. If I wanted to have steady confidence and a
strong sense of balance, I needed more knowledge, or, better said,
knowledge reorganized. I needed to clearly see something I could
work with, that I could trust, trust in the sense it could take me
where I wanted to go. And that strong desire eventually led to the
knowledge highlighted in this book.

While all the material I eventually gathered to me is important,
the lynchpin holding it all together is action and the three creative
dilemmas of All That Is. If I had not re-found that information in
my quest for renewed knowledge, I still would not have understood how the subsequent pieces—from the spacious present
through the entity/inner self—so clearly identify the whole, how
they are not simply fascinating standalone bits of information, but
are absolutely crucial to the *logical* flow of creation. Therefore, I
still would not have seen a path forward into lasting trust, because
it is the whole that shows why our trust is fully warranted.

So, step one was under my belt—I now had my knowledge.
What then?

Building Trust in the Moment Point

Knowledge is magnificent. It is expanding and freeing. But by now we know knowledge is only half of the trust pie. The other half is *becoming* that knowledge, integrating it so thoroughly into the fabric of our being that it cannot be seen as separate from our self. In order to accomplish this feat, we must work with what we know to be true of the self, not hold on to outmoded ideas that no longer apply and do nothing but hobble our growth. And one thing we unequivocally know is that we use the moment point to constantly create, and re-create, our self and our environment—which are actually one and the same—through our expectation and suggestion. Ergo, we must learn to *trust* the moment point in order to use it. Step two, in other words. (Although in actuality, both sides of the trust pie, knowledge and integration, are worked concurrently.)

The one truth that will make or break our use of the moment point (its acceptance or rejection being the defining issue) is that *we expand from our center*. Quite literally, in fact. That is, the growth, or value fulfillment, of consciousness starts at its core and projects itself outward into all aspects of that consciousness, forever changing itself into a greater embodiment of itself, not in size, but in value fulfillment. It all happens in the moment point, the only time there is. And what is growth to consciousness? Changes brought about by action. And what drives action? Suggestion/expectation, or mental acts.

Do you see where this is going? And how important it is to us? We must *practically*, as well as intellectually, accept that, no matter what linear time tells us, we are re-creating and expanding our self from our center in each of our moment points *by what we ex-pect and suggest*, and the emotions behind it. That is not to say our suggestions and expectations are immediately reflected in our personal reality, although that can happen. But it is to say our inner self uses those suggestions and expectations in some way in coming events.

This, then, is the basis for the new method of thinking we must incorporate. By either embracing or ignoring this knowledge, we do not change the fact that we create, moment by moment, from our center, expanding outward; and we do not change the fact of the moment point's power. It is what it is. In my opinion, the only way to consistently live a safe universe is to make the choice to embrace and use it.

So, working with the moment point in order to consciously influence our reality—which is what we want to do—will butt heads with the cause and effect belief, because the beliefs are incompatible. At best, holding both of them could lead to some measure of relief from our haphazard and unenlightened constructions, as it did for me in the nineties, but is that all we want out of our reality? Absolutely not, and that means our trust in the moment point and the simultaneous nature of time has to trump our belief in cause and effect in linear time.

The crux of what we have to come to trust is this: Since physical reality is subjective, it means we have great sway over it through our emotions, imaginings and thoughts—our subjective states of mind, in other words. Which further means, since our subjective states are generated by us, we can consciously implement them in order to secure our moment point. And the emotional environment of our moment point is absolutely crucial to the quality, if you will, of what we create, so it must be understood and consciously implemented, along with the application of thoughts.

So, how do we learn to practically apply our knowledge to the moment point? Initially, I found this to be quite a dilemma, because, in retrospect, I chose the incorrect starting point—and it didn't work out all that well. Where I started was with my thoughts. I jumped right in to the learning process by attempting to feed positive thoughts into the moments during reflective quiet times, or any other times I chose. Some of the thoughts were short Seth quotes, some were my goals, and others a potpourri of other ideas I thought would help. And while they all meant a lot to me, they never fully developed within me the consistent feeling of living a safe universe, or the trust it took to do so.

Finally, through trial and error, I found a path and used it. What I had needed to do all along was first shake the false mental barriers of space and time to their roots, so I could better sense my continuous place in the spacious present through my moment points. Once that was accomplished, I could move on to other ways of re-framing my thinking so it was compatible with simultaneous time instead of linear time/cause and effect.

Below are listed several tasks I undertook along the way which, for me, were essential basics, those needed to start the turning of my mind away from the belief in linear time, instead to the truth of simultaneous time. It seems so clear now that I needed to first get the sense that, while seeming objective, *physical reality is completely subjective*. Without that sense, not just my intellectual knowledge, I would not have been able to shed the ramifications of my belief in cause and effect. And if I had not made headway into changing my cause-and-effect mindset, I could not have ultimately used my mind consciously to work within the simultaneous time of the moment point.

So, the tasks I undertook to help me were meant to be twofold: to build within me a sense of simultaneous time and my constantly forming physical reality; and to consciously learn to use my mind and emotions in the moment point. They are, in essence, to help me consciously use the moment point as my gateway to creation, and in so doing, break the unquestioned bond to a belief in a linear past and future. I offer them to you below.

A note before we proceed: I mentioned earlier that for years I studied beliefs and tried to change ones that were not to my benefit. It worked to a point, but the whole process did not lead me to full trust. If anything, it highlighted the difficulty of seriously changing my reality if working with beliefs was all I did, because beliefs form, and re-form, in the moment points (when else would they?). Which meant they slid in unnoticed at times, because I was pretty much blind to their formation, development or return in the moment point, because I was blind to the moment point and its power—they were, to me, simply thoughts.

So, my focus on a search for trust led me to recognize a very different path through the Seth material that I could use instead. Perhaps you will choose to give that path a try too, once you can see it fully presented here. However, if you have never worked at finding and changing your beliefs, I strongly recommend you spend some quality time with a belief search-and-change effort concurrently or before you proceed to what I'll be suggesting. It's an excellent way to learn so much about yourself, such as how and why you've been creating the reality you have to date. I think I'd even consider it a prerequisite to substantial change, because of the great amount of insights into reality creation you'll amass along the way. If you feel it's a path worth exploring, and you'd appreciate or need assistance in your belief work, two of my books—*Beyond the Winning Streak: Using Conscious Creation to Consistently Win at Life* and *Ten Thousand Whispers: A Guide to Conscious Creation*—between them cover finding and changing beliefs, as well as other Seth subjects about conscious creation, in depth.

Task #1 – Seeing Beyond Camouflage Constructions:

One of the first tasks I undertook to help me get a sense of the moment point has to do with camouflage constructions. We know our physical reality is created through the illusion of camouflage, and is re-created millions of times a second. We also know it never leaves the spacious present. And we know the only creations we experience in our physical reality are those we can see, touch, smell, hear or taste.

So, here's what I do. I sit in my living room with eyes open, absorbing the realization that the room and everything in it is being re-created millions of times a second—it is there and then not there, and back again. And I think about the fact that nothing is beyond its walls except the spacious present. There is no camouflage beyond the walls because I cannot <u>see</u> it; therefore, it is not manifest into camouflage—not the outside environment, other than what shows through the windows; not the other rooms in my home. So, I visualize seeing <u>nothing</u> beyond the walls, knowing what I see of the room is the only camouflage currently present in my physical reality. And when a car drives by that I cannot see, I realize *there is no physical car*, only the sound of one.

Then I close my eyes and know all the camouflage quite literally disappears. Only what I touch is now manifest, such as the couch I sit on. But the couch is not manifest as a whole physical object, simply the place of my *touch* is manifest, because I cannot *see or feel* the rest of it.

I do this task while walking or driving too. I think about the fact that the road, sidewalk or beach have nothing underneath them but the non-camouflaged spacious present. I know the speed of my car, or the speed of my feet, is only a *perception* created within my camouflage reality. How can I actually be moving through space and time when neither exists?

Task #2 – Recognizing What I See as My Reality:

Here's another task I use, one I now know to be a most truthfully realistic and accurate assessment of my reality. This time I don't necessarily want to see beyond the camouflage, but instead to *embrace* the whole of what I see as my reality.

So, wherever I am, be it by the ocean or in a grocery store, I look around and know *everything I'm viewing is my reality, and <u>only</u> mine.* No one else creates this same reality, because *they are not in my dimension of existence.* And I am at the center of my reality, it emanates from within my core. Every bit of it, from the sun, to the people, to the shelves stocked with goods, is my physical creation, including what I perceive as space. I also know that only what I see, touch, smell, hear or taste is manifest. Therefore, there is nothing behind me until I turn around and look at it, not people in the grocery store, indeed not that part of the store itself. So, while driving, when I glance in my rearview mirror, I know *there is nothing behind me*, no matter what shows in the mirror. I must turn around and see it first, and then it will enter my reality.

Task #3 – Tying Events to Emotions:

Another task I undertook was an exercise in awareness of how moods create—not of how events create moods, but of how emotions, action that they are, create experiences. As part of my education about moment points, I felt I needed to be able to recognize the creative force of emotions as they are reflected within my events—and make no mistake, they always are. And also make no mistake, every event expressed in my reality can be called <u>mine</u>, even if it's between two strangers and I am but a bystander. All events have an emotional coloration to them, some not so much, some loaded with it, but since all events are mine, it's *my* emotions I'm looking for, not someone else's. It can be no other way, based on how I, as consciousness, create my reality.

So, a brawl I witness between two strangers is <u>my</u> event, and can become a significant teaching experience for me, since my emotions are there for me to understand and learn from. And obviously what I'm taking from my learning is *how my emotions influence what I experience*. So, my task is to search my heart and mind for how I *felt*, not what I thought, prior to, during and after an event. Perhaps what I felt had nothing whatsoever to do with what the event externally says to me—my symbols (such as a brawl) are private to me and can't really be figured out by another, or by what might be considered by some common sense cause-and-effect analysis.

But it's not only the big events I'd analyze as I proceeded in my learning. It could be the smile of a stranger, a change in atmospheric conditions, a phone call just in the nick of time, a rude driver, an unhelpful store clerk, good or poor restaurant food. I took note of what happened to me and whether I'd been obviously happy, sad, doubtful, fearful, buoyant, or whatever. And eventually I started to see the tie-in of events to my emotions.

Task #4 – Learning to Use the Creative Force of Emotion:

Now that I felt I could usually recognize the creative force of emotion in my events, and see how it played out, I decided I could learn to use it, to direct it in my favor. I wanted nothing less than to set the emotional environment for *all* of my moment points. In other words, I wanted to create a beneficial state of emotion that, to the best of my ability, I could hold going forward into each moment point.

So, my next task was to learn to stay happy. I'm not kidding, that's what I decided. When you think about it, what better moment point emotional environment could I offer myself for the best possible creations? The kind of happy I'm talking about is fully identified with my self, though. It does not come from an outside source or event, ever. It is there because I am there. And I am there because I know exactly what I'm doing in seeking happiness in the moment, what my purpose is, and what my results will be because of it. Besides, it feels good.

So, this task is simple. I smile for no apparent reason, and relax into it. I know my happy moment point creates the fertile emotional environment in the spacious present upon which my upcoming creations will reside. Therefore, I know a happy, relaxed moment point is one of the most valuable gifts I can give myself. So, I simply smile and become happy. And if I forget to feel happy long enough for stress in any form to enter a moment point, no problem. I smile again, and relax into it—or give it my best shot.

The same technique works for other emotions I wish to experience too. For instance, a sense of calm. Or clear or strong or balanced, or whatever it is I'm aiming for in that moment.

Okay, "happy" was not a slam dunk. It took a lot of trial and error to reach somewhat sustainable happy (sporadic happy is no problem), and it didn't really have a chance to fully bloom until I pulled together the material in this book, because being rather consistently happy, I found, takes trust—trust in the nature of reality and the power of simultaneous time. For me, it was like the gift at the end of the long evolution of self.

But two things I want to say here. First, "consistently happy" doesn't mean every moment is covered. What it means to me is, if I lose it here and there, I can usually wiggle back into it with an ease now born of experience. And second, consistently happy is only waiting for trust. If trust is quick in coming, so is consistently happy. If finding trust is a long process, like it was for me, it could push consistently happy out somewhat. I'm sincerely hoping my book will help you make it happen sooner rather than later, if it hasn't happened yet.

Task #5 – Recognizing Free-Flowing Thoughts:

Seth said earlier, "Each mental act is a reality for which you are responsible," and by now it's clear why. (Remember, mental acts are thoughts, emotions and imaginings.) It is one of the reasons happy works so well—it's a mental act which influences reality. I put this task #5 in place, then, to explore the mental acts of my unfettered thoughts, the ones I didn't realize were doing so much creating because I didn't give them my conscious awareness; the ones I was responsible for, because *thinking them meant they became some part of my reality.*

So I started by writing down random thoughts, or at times simply acknowledging that I heard them. I took special interest in what I thought on the downside of my supposed past. You know, the thoughts and memories (which are, themselves, thoughts emotion and imagining) that reveal doubt, hurt, anger, sadness, hopelessness, etc. And the reason I was so interested in seeing them was so I would become aware of what I was doing, and *stop replaying them over and over again* in my moment points. Like Seth says, "If you constantly focus on the belief that your early background was damaging and negative, then only such experiences will flow into your present life from the past."[3]

And what about my thoughts of the future, let's say a dire future? What if I projected into the moment point the thought that things could only get worse instead of better? That there was no solution for what was to come? Or that I was held back from the future of my choice because of circumstances such as education or age or sex? I mean, how dumb would I be if, in spite of what I know now about moment point creation, I'd still continue along those tracks?

But I didn't only want to see my less than stellar thoughts and memories; I was also very much interested in ones that showcased my strengths. Those, I obviously wanted to build upon. Which takes me to the next task.

Task #6 – Learning to Use the Creative Force of Thought:

The moment point is where we offer up what we want out of life to our inner self for help with its fulfillment. It's where we state what we see as our future, our trust it can be accomplished, and our enthusiasm for life in general. Our future, in other words, rests securely in our moment point thinking…and our future includes the immediate moment points within each day as well as our longer range goals. Learning to use thought in the moment point, as well as emotion, is the answer to breaking the belief of linear time/cause and effect over our lives.

A comment Seth made earlier was, "You must become consciously aware of what you tell yourself is true every moment of the day, for that is the reality that you project outward." Certainly the previous task of recognizing past thoughts and memories that constantly re-form themselves into the future applies nicely to that comment. This time, however, we're talking about developing thoughts by choice, not just recognizing what's there already.

One of the first things I did to help me along was place that comment of Seth's on signs around my home. I wanted a constant reminder of how crucial what I thought in my moment points was to the creation of my reality, how true they became.

Then, over the years, I did several things, two of which are listed here. I hope they will be helpful to you.

* I gathered to me hundreds of short Seth quotes that reinforce such things as how the nature of reality works, how and why my inner self assists in the process, Seth's advice on how to change my reality, the pitfalls to avoid, the benefits to it all, etc.

I formed these quotes into documents anywhere from, on average, one to four pages in length, and titled each of them. One title I used a lot for different sets of quotes was "What Would Seth Say to Me Today?" Many were more specific, such as "What Would Seth Say to Me Today About Solving Problems?" And "What Would Seth Say to Me Today About Trust?" Others included "Consciously Creating My Moment Points," "Working with Probabilities," "Seth on a Safe Universe," etc.

Once a document was created, I used it to focus on the need at hand, and eventually added it to my whole pile of documents. I keep them handy to this day, and either pick one randomly or by purpose to read again and think about. If I had to point to any one overall act of mine that has had the most influence on my reaching trust, perhaps it is my Seth quotes docs. They focus the material into information that is specific to my needs of the current moment point. It is as though Seth is talking privately to me, helping, counseling, rapping my knuckles at times. Seth comes alive in my reality through my docs in a way he could not, for me, simply by reading the books.

* I created a several page document called "Framing My Spacious Present Moment Point." Below the title, I write several words that capture what I want most to feel in each of my moment points. (The words change over time, as my needs change.) Then I add some comments of my own, and follow with several Seth quotes that bring clarity to how and why I might want to experience my moment points a certain way (both of which also change over time).

To explain this document, I'll create a rough facsimile of one below, and then I'll follow with how I use it.

*** Framing My Spacious Present Moment Point***

Happy

Clear

Calm

Trusting

UNIMPEDED

*****

I project my reality from my center in this NOW – the only time there is.

**

For the first time, I understand my job in relation to my inner self's job. I clear my moment points, which gives us the best possible conditions for our joint growth, and then offer my choice of direction. And IS then creates the circumstances and experiences that bring us the most value fulfillment.

****

Seth Comments

Miracles are nature unimpeded. [4]

**

If you direct your inner self with confidence to steer you through your physical existence, it will do so. If you concentrate upon difficulties, you will not allow it to do so. For any <u>negative</u> focus within egotistical reality will automatically block you. [5]

**

Live each moment as fully and joyfully as possible. Imaging the best possible results of any plans or projects. Above all, do not concentrate upon past unfavorable events, or imagined future ones. You can make plans for the future, but do not worry about the future. Live each moment. [6]

**

You translate what you are into an event that you can understand. [7]

**

You cannot concentrate upon two things at once. So to the extent that you concentrate upon your pleasures, your accomplishments, and to the extent that you relate to the psychic and biological moment, you are refreshing yourselves. You are not projecting negatively, and you are allowing the problem to unwrinkle, unknot. [8]

(Etc. folks)

What I do with this constantly evolving document is to use it to snap me into the moment point. I envision a box, similar to the one above, around everything my eyes see within my forward vision. This represents my reality. Within my reality box, I think of my first highlighted word, in this case "happy." And I feel myself happy, giving it time to develop and to be enjoyed. Then I go on to the second word, "clear," and do the same. I then read my own comments, reflecting on their specific meaning to me, and follow with the perusal of my Seth quotes, or a portion of them. All of this is done with a slowness, an absorption within the moment point. I take this document on quiet walks, on airplanes, wherever. It's not at all meant to stay at home, simply used in psy-times. But it *is* meant to be absorbed, whatever the circumstances, if possible.

Task #7 – Learning to Use the Creative Force of Imagining:

As Seth said earlier, "True imagination dares to speculate upon that which is not yet." The last of the mental acts (not including dreams, which we're not covering in this book), also comes to us with great power. When we think of the past and automatically put imaginative pictures to it, we give it emphasis in the Now—which means we dare to speculate upon that which is not yet. The same thing happens with the future. So, we must choose wisely where we place our imagination, and reign it in when we realize it's dwelling on past or future events that we really do not want to meet in our projected reality.

Our imaginations are active constantly, not just in specific focuses like visualization, so it becomes a moment-by-moment awareness, if necessary, to keep them creating wisely for us. I found there's a naturalness to imaging, in that it so easily follows my thoughts and emotions—up or down. So what I do is simply reinforce an image that is tied to a thought or memory, or drop it, if appropriate. For instance, when an imaged scene is reinforcing my doubts or concerns, I tone it down. What I also found was when I make that conscious choice to tone the imagining down or drop it, it automatically tones down my thoughts and emotions that could lead me astray, or entirely removes the whole issue from my thoughts; and the opposite happens on the upside, of course.

It could be said our imagination gives substance to our thoughts and emotions, drawing them even closer to actuality. Ergo, to use the power of our moment point imaginations is to consciously create our reality more closely to what we wish to experience.

A note before we continue with the wrap up below: None of the tasks I mention above worked all of the time for me. Sometimes I just felt dull. Nothing would click, nothing would hold. Nothing helped me remember the moment point, let alone consciously live it. I did my best to bounce back quickly, but sometimes the feeling of disconnect dragged on. I just want you to know that, in case the same thing happens to you. Hang in there, it will all work out.

Task #8 – An Example of Wrapping It All Together: My Health in the Moment Point

So, that's it, folks, some of the basic ingredients, or tasks, I wrapped into my efforts to live safely in my reality. Moment point thinking has become my mode of operation a good portion of the time, and I wonder at my blindness to it for so many years. One of the issues that could have helped me in my learning, had I but seen it as significant, was my health. I could have used it as an example of how moment point thinking works well, but until rather recently I didn't even notice—I simply took my thinking for granted. And yet I was naturally using everything positive in the moment point, from emotion to thoughts and imaginings. Here's what I mean, and I offer it to you as the wrap up to my Task section.

Okay, as of the publication date of this book, I have not visited a doctor since I was 44, which was in 1987, with the one exception being a 15-minute drop-in to a local clinic for a minor issue. I stopped health insurance in 1989. The only drug or medication I have used since that time is Tylenol. I've never had a mammogram, Pap smear, cholesterol or cardiovascular test, or any other medical test. I am so out of the loop, medically speaking, my daughter recently had to explain the term "co-pay" to me.

I wish I could take credit for creating my health through consciously focused thought—it would make a great story, I do believe. But I cannot. As mentioned earlier, I started reading the Seth material in 1984, and while it played a role in my final leap to medical freedom, as an adult I'd very seldom been sick anyway. When I decided to take a look at my mindset toward my health, the learning came not from what I had consciously accomplished as a goal, but rather through what I had accomplished with no conscious effort. And to me it now speaks volumes about how very well I use the moment point in this instance.

For example, here's some of what I do, or don't do, as the case may be, naturally:

* I never project illness into the future. In fact, it quite literally never occurs to me that something could possibly make me ill.

* The same goes for potential accidents. That I could harm myself in some way which would require a doctor's visit is not within my realm of thinking. And I never imagine a potential accident (such

as when walking down stairs).

* I never say I'm sick in order to get out of a commitment or garner sympathy. Actually, I don't say it at all, for any reason.

* I don't choose foods for their supposedly healthy components. I am a vegetarian, but it is not for health reasons—it's all about the animals.

* I don't drink water. In a year, I'm guessing I might down a total of five glasses, and maybe that's a stretch.

* I don't take preventative measures, such as using antibacterial soap or sunscreen. The reality is I could not care less about them.

* I never read health-related articles or watch programs on health or illness. My disinterest is total.

* I only have a very vague idea of where organs are found in my body, or their purposes. Nor do I care.

* I don't watch TV commercials, which spare me the bombardment by Big Pharma. I stopped watching television in 1969, and only picked it up again in 2003. But never do I watch live TV, only what's recorded on my DVR, which, of course, means I can fast-forward through commercials.

* I have no idea where hospitals or clinics are located unless they

are on my beaten path. It's not that I don't occasionally drive by them in neighboring towns, it's that they simply don't register with me.

* I sincerely appreciate my body. It's been good to me and deserves every ounce of appreciation I give it.

* I believe my body will let me know what it needs. For instance, I don't as a rule take vitamins. But if I feel I'm being nudged toward them, I'll acquiesce until the feeling recedes.

* I walk. I've been a walker for most of my adult life (a runner at times too, with one marathon, the New York, under my belt). I almost always grab a page of short Seth quotes on my way out the door to think about during my private, pleasant, focused-time walks.

* When I do have an occasional ache or pain, I don't see it as a health issue. My mind holds it where it is, because I don't build it up as the precursor to something worse.

An aside: Seth says any serious illness is due to a feeling of powerlessness. He also says lesser illnesses can be kicked off by tangential beliefs, such as a belief that not getting a flu shot has left one vulnerable to flu. When all is said and done, though, can't all illnesses and other kinds of manifested unsafe conditions be ascribed to some level of feeling powerless, simply because powerlessness engenders fear? Which then translates itself into outcomes in our personal realities?

And here's an interesting comment from Seth which can be extrapolated to cover how our beliefs about health create our realities in the general area of wellness: "In many instances people exercise quite simply because they are afraid of what will happen if they do not. They may run to avoid heart disease, for example, while their own fear can help to promote the very eventuality they fear. ... It is true that the reason that you exercise is actually more important than the exercises that you do perform. The reason can promote your good health or actually impede it."[9]

Tips, Thoughts and Other Miscellaneous Musings

For the rest of this chapter, I offer you one personal story and some musings, tips, Seth quotes, and comments I've made to Seth friends on my Facebook page that I hope, overall, will have some meaning to you as they pertain to reality creation in the moment point. They are in no particular order, and with no particular emphasis on anything other than another way of understanding the power of using the moment point, or the knowledge behind why we can trust it. I hope you enjoy them, but more, I hope they clarify for you ways you can strengthen your own ideas about trust in simultaneous time, thereby helping you to live more safely in your reality, if needed.

A Personal Story...

I said earlier the Seth material played a role in my final leap to medical freedom. The understanding that my self is formed and held in the spacious present and then projected into physical reality millions of times a second, and that each event serves a purpose, changes completely how I interact with it. To me it means solutions to problems or issues must reside in my subjective reality, not my objectified one, and I believe this so strongly it defined how I once reacted to a potential death experience.

It was a couple years after Stan's passing, when I was still raw and worn down from the events of those intervening years. One night I started having strong pain in my left arm and my heart quite literally ached. I had known for a long time my "heart" was still psychologically near breaking, and because of that knowledge, I intuitively knew I was making a choice to live or die. I had no idea what the outcome would be, but I well understood what was going on psychically.

So, holding my left arm close to my aching chest, I filled my cats' water and food bowls and sat in my Kennedy rocker, the chair in which I had rocked my babies many decades earlier. At some point, I crawled under the bedcovers. If I slept, I thought, I'd either wake up dead or alive, and I did not consciously care which one: Both had their advantages. It would have to get sorted out in the spacious present between my inner self and me.

Sometime during the night the pain started to recede and finally stopped. The choice to continue living had obviously been made.

A Musing...

Trust seems hard to come by in this reality when bad things happen. And as Seth readers, we often attempt to understand why they occurred. We look to the past, to our beliefs, to our thoughts, searching for patterns and answers. But what we sometimes cannot see is how those events play into the overall picture of our life, what their meaning and purpose is on a broader, grander scale, and it bothers us or leaves us shaken. But maybe we simply shouldn't care, maybe we should just drop it instead.

Seth says, "You cannot rip apart your events to find the reality behind them, for that reality is not so much a glue that holds events together, but is invisibly entwined within your own psychological being."[10] And, "In that <u>larger picture</u> there are no errors, for each action, pleasant or not, will in its fashion be redeemed, both in relation to itself and…to a larger picture that the conscious mind may not be able presently to perceive."[11]

To live a safe universe takes a profound belief in, and trust of, our self, as well as a trust that the events we create are on purpose—*our* purpose. We only chip away at the trust we're building if we see it any other way. It's simply not worth it. So, my answer: Drop the doubt and move on.

Seth…

"I am not telling you to examine your thoughts so frequently and with such vigor that you get in your own way, but you are not fully conscious unless you are aware of the contents of your conscious mind."[12]

A Musing…

Been sitting here thinking about the raging debate going on today by people who believe in a god outside themselves and the cause and effect of linear time—in other words complete separation between them and, well, everything else. And I'm also thinking of how divisive a belief in separation can be, not only in this context, but in any number of arenas of world thought. And I'm wondering what a world would be like where people actually understood the nature of consciousness. Where they understood about significances and purpose and meaning. And then I'm thinking that Seth says something we, as the human race, should seriously consider: We've taken our belief in separation as far as we can without destroying ourselves.

And finally, I'm thinking about this one line of Seth's, given earlier: "It is only through the recognition of the inner self that the race of man will ever use its potential." To me, intrinsically woven within its full meaning is the answer to all my ponderings.

A Comment to a Facebook Friend...

"I'd like to suggest something that, for me, made a world of difference. You said, 'Believing in a safe universe requires overcoming the universal survival fears that lead to adversity and conflict.' That was my thinking too, for more years than I care to count.

"Long story, but here's my recommendation: Don't focus on eradicating individual fear/conflict beliefs per se. Instead, focus on the consciousness that you are, not the physical self you believe you are, and learn to use the tools used by all consciousness. See yourself differently, not in linear time facing cause and effect, but in the spacious present creating a camouflage reality from your action, moment by moment. The difference in those positions is startling, when you think about it. One takes control of your mental climate, one leaves you floundering without life support."

A Tip...

Remember, our subjectivity is what brings continuity to our experiences, not a time sequence. To explain it from a practical perspective, think about a present belief in victimization. A belief is subjective, as are all mental acts, so a present belief in victimization sets up the supposed past with events that mirror the belief. And, oh so helpfully, it also sets up the future to reflect the belief. That's called, by Seth, subjective continuity. So, break the continuity, change the past.

That's quite literally how spontaneous faith healings occur. To explain, Seth says, "A sudden or intense belief in health can indeed 'reverse' a disease, but in a very practical way it is a reversal in terms of time."[13] A new belief in the present breaks old continuity to the past, and voilà, a new past emerges. It has to, because the new belief is action, and action terminates the previous action, creating a new reality with its own past and future.

Seth...

"Faith in a creative, fulfilling, desired end—sustained faith—literally draws from Framework 2 all of the necessary ingredients, all of the elements however staggering in number, all the details, and then inserts into Framework 1 the impulses, dreams, chance meetings, motivations, or whatever is necessary so that the desired end then falls into place as a completed pattern."[14]

A Comment to Facebook Friends...

"My feeling about aging is that there is an integrity to it, and with it comes a sense of accomplishment. Not accomplishment in normally used terms, but an accomplishment of consciousness. Physically being what it came here to be, expressing itself in material form through all of its physical aspects. I'm quite content with aging."

Added later: My beliefs about aging are similar to my beliefs about health: They're all in the background, and none of them are harmful. Since death is not an issue with me, and since I know I constantly create my own reality in the moment point, including my body, I'm good.

Here's some of what I do, or don't do, naturally:

- I was born in 1943, yet my age today means no more or less to me than ages 30 or 55. I don't think of age per se, but as an expansion of my consciousness in the spacious present.

- I see no advantage, or disadvantage, to youth. To me, it's simply a state of consciousness seeking its own value fulfillment, as all states of consciousness are.

- I don't see or think of myself as "senior." It never enters my mind to categorize myself as such.

- I read no articles or watch programs on aging.

- I eat no differently to "compensate" for aging.

- I use no "anti-aging" creams, medications, or such.

- I take no precautions of any sort that suggest aging is a different state than natural.

- I never use age as an excuse.

- I never say to family or friends comments such as, "I'm getting old." It never occurs to me to do so, because "old" has lost its mental or psychic relevancy to me.

To close this comment on aging, I give you Seth: "The experiences you may encounter in your sixties are as necessary as those in your twenties. Your changing image is supposed to <u>tell</u> you something. When you pretend alterations do not occur you block both biological and spiritual messages."[15]

A Tip...

A most difficult lesson for me to learn was to trust all events—good, bad or indifferent, as I might classify them. Seth says, "Every event serves a purpose. Every event is offered for a reason. What is good? What is bad?" Easy for him to say, I used to think, he's not the one living them!

Eons ago, when I was still new to it all, I thought my inner self was presenting me with a "learning experience" when something unsettling would occur. But that doesn't work too well over the long run, as I found out. How does one build trust if they believe: a) they have no overt participation in the creation of the "learning experience," because their learning is being controlled by something outside themselves, even if it's called inner self; and b) God only knows what might be thrown at them next.

Eventually, I bought wholly into the idea that I actively participate with my inner self in the selection of what I experience. But then, alas, I started to direct the blame game toward myself. I'd "failed" yet again to change from the old to the new, as I saw it, if something occurred that was upsetting. Which only held off my experiencing trust, because how could I trust myself under those conditions?

I finally got over the self-imposed hurdles, but it didn't happen until I fully pulled my inner self into the "I" equation along with me. I had to realize, emotionally as well as intellectually, that we truly are one, and our decisions are with purpose. And, as importantly, that my inner self frequently sends me thoughts and images, as well as inspiration and impulses, to help me along.

My tip to you: Trust is too precious to let false beliefs keep us from it.

Seth...

"If you cannot trust that which keeps you alive, then what can you trust?"[16]

A Comment to a Facebook Friend...

"Just before I read your two posts, I was writing something for my upcoming book, trying to find the words to express how, for me, attempting to mesh what I knew to be true about simultaneous time and the spacious present into my linear time framework of cause-and-effect thinking was the most difficult thing I've ever done. And your posts reflect perfectly my own feelings of that dilemma. My own consternation eventually forced me to find a path out of one method of thinking and into another one—it was either that or...well, there was no "or." To survive, I had to.

"My tip to you: Give up on trying to figure things out as though you're in linear time with its cause and effect. Instead look at <u>everything</u> from the standpoint of you being consciousness in the spacious present, continually creating from your center in the Now. And I mean everything, otherwise things can get murky and confused between the two rather quickly, weakening your clarity and resolve instead of strengthening it."

A Musing...

When we start thinking about our probable pasts and how to choose one over another, we're still thinking of linear time versus spacious present. What I mean is, I believe our focus has to be clearly in the present, not worried about or consciously attempting to choose <u>any</u> past. Our present mindset does its own selection of the past naturally, right? So, all we have to care about is knowing what we think in the present. Then the past (and future) falls in line naturally. It <u>has</u> to, according to Seth, so that's our answer to changing our past.

A Comment to Facebook Friends...

"I'm always hesitant to bring up the subject of beliefs here, and have only done so a small handful of times. And yet we know how important they are, right? My dilemma is this: Beliefs are normally thought of from a linear time perspective. We think they were created in the past, and we think they will impact our future, or at least have the capacity to do so. In other words, we almost always lay them out <u>through time</u> in our thinking. You guys see the downside here?

"My personal bottom line: Beliefs, when broken down into their components of thought, emotion and imagination, can be handled in the present as they enter that moment point. And I think it's far easier than any other way. A caveat: We have to trust our self, or we won't trust the process."

Seth...

"There is a steady, even flow in which your conscious activity through the neurological structure brings about events, and a familiar pattern of reaction is established. When you alter these conscious beliefs through effort, then a period of time is necessary while the structure learns to adjust to the new preferred situation. If beliefs are changed overnight, then comparatively less time is required."[17]

A Musing...

I specifically kept this book focused on the individual, because it's about redefining and trusting the self. Therefore, mass events are not addressed, and I only briefly touch on the spacious present interaction between individuals preparing a scene for a shared camouflage event through telepathy.

But what I do want to say, in case there's even the slightest doubt in your mind, is that we are never dragged into an experience by another person or mass event without our acquiescence. In a very concrete way, we are at the center of our own universe within our own dimension of existence; therefore, we call the shots as to what we'll experience, right down to the conversation with our neighbor, and the creation of the 10,000 seat concert hall we visit, stuffed to the rafters with people.

So, when the bottom line is reached, it really is all about each of us individually. Not in a selfish way, but realistically.

A Tip...

Regarding supposed unconscious beliefs: As Seth tells us, we can't be tripped up by some hidden belief, because beliefs aren't hidden at all. They're part of our psyches, and our psyches are what are reflected back to us in our experiences. Watch our experiences (and what we say and write about them); see our beliefs. What seems to hide them is simply our lack of awareness, or maybe our lack of understanding about what creates our reality and why. But once we're clear that beliefs are not hidden, we're home free.

A Comment to Facebook Friends...

"I think it's good for us to remember we really are pioneers of consciousness, and pioneering comes with a built-in necessity for learning and applying. Ah, but then those magical frontiers of the psyche, the ones that can bring us great fulfillment, become ours for the conquering."

A Musing...

Seth tells us, "You must be willing to change all the way from the old system of orientation to the new, if you want the new approach to work fully for you in your lives."[18] In my opinion, we serious Seth readers need to up our game a little. It's time to go beyond the basics, to truly get a far better grasp on what Seth is saying about consciousness and the nature of reality from a spacious present standpoint; and then use that knowledge.

We have a unique opportunity to quite literally help flesh out what will eventually become a major change to our world. We're the first line, ragged and shattered at times as we are. But we're trying and, as importantly, learning. And we should never settle for less, no Seth lite. We should stand tall, proud of what we know and how we're doing our best to integrate it in a world that believes in linear time/cause and effect, and a god outside themselves. We each chose to be unique. So let's run with it.

The Final Word Goes to Seth...

"Organize your reality according to your strength; organize your reality according to your playfulness; according to your dreams; according to your joy; according to your hopes—and *then* you can help those who organize their realities according to their fears."[19]

12

You live in a safe universe. This is not only a valid psychic truth, but is the basis for cellular integrity.
—*Seth,* Deleted Session, 10/06/75

Living Safely With
Conscious Understanding

What constitutes an unsafe universe? If All That Is had perfected an unsafe universe as the model for its creations, what would it look like? One of the most obvious frameworks of such a universe would be an abundance of fear, since that's the emotion engendered by the belief in a lack of safety. And that would be closely followed by the creation of seemingly endless protections against all that is feared. With fears and protections in place, the consciousness inhabiting such a model could go unhappily about the business of creating its reality.

But, All That Is instead created a safe universe, one devoid of the need to fear, where protections are not necessary for the safe-framework model, and one where consciousness could go happily about the business of creating its reality.

Seth tells us we live in a safe universe, and he tells us this is a psychic truth. He's not saying, however, our personal universe is always seen as safe, simply because we have the free will to play at not being safe, if it suits our needs (i.e. resonates with our beliefs). But underneath our creations is a reality of complete safety, always inviolate.

So, which do we choose, a safe universe or an unsafe one? As Seth asks us, "Which you? Which world?" He says, "When people are convinced that the self is untrustworthy, for whatever reasons, or that the universe is not safe, then instead of luxuriating in the use of their abilities, exploring the physical and mental environments, they begin to pull in their realities—to contract their abilities, to over-control their environments. They become frightened people."[1]

So, fear is definitely the issue that needs to be resolved in order to live safely, and not just a fear here and there, but a whole new mindset that scoffs at the idea of fear. Our personal safe universe is of our own making, but we can't take it half way and expect to live a reality free of fear. As Seth says, "You cannot equivocate.... You cannot say, 'I live in a safe universe but but' anything. ... The threat will follow you and erupt in one way or another...."[2]

Believing in a safe universe is a first step for us, albeit a *huge* first step. It immediately eliminates the belief in outside forces harming us—whether those forces are people, events, strange powers or, not insignificantly, even the past. It puts the responsibility of non-safety squarely on our shoulders—which is exactly where it needs to be. How else can we change unpleasant circumstances unless we take responsibility for their creation? And how very fortunate are we to have such a get-out-of-jail-free card? We must truly believe we have the ability to change our circumstances. Why? Because we <u>can</u>.

According to Seth, "When you thoroughly understand what is meant by the entire safe universe concept, then the physical, cultural climate is seen as a medium through which the ideal can be expressed. The ideal is meaningless if it is not physically manifest to one degree or another. The ideal <u>seeks</u> expression."[3]

So, it's up to each of us as to which world we choose to inhabit, the one that is basic to the safe nature of the universe, or the one that is unnaturally created in line with our fears. Whichever we choose, we are responsible for its expression in our realities, because the ideal, or idea, is always expressed.

The Final Recap

When all of Seth's words are read and absorbed, when all of the intricacies of his statements clarified, his bottom line message is clear: We honestly do live in a safe universe. It is a message of such startling proportions and certitude we stand in awe of its scope of possibilities, for ourselves and for our world.

And then what seems to be reality sets in, a moment at a time. We fully believe Seth—that is definitely not the issue. The issue, for many of us, is we know we live in a safe universe, no problem; it's just that our personal universe, our own reality, doesn't always reflect safety. We're still creating those haphazard and unenlightened constructions Seth talks about, the ones that take us under, that seem to harm our way of life, that reflect depression or illness or desperation or hopelessness. The ones that come from a belief in cause and effect and some force outside ourselves that can impact us.

And that is *exactly* where they come from. The underlying issue that causes our unenlightened constructions is our acceptance of linear time, and all the beliefs that flow from it. Or, perhaps better said, our non-conscious use of subjective time. Because on one level, we soundly reject the idea of linear time/cause and effect—we know it's a fallacy, constructed as a camouflage framework for physical reality. It's just that we haven't trained ourselves sufficiently to change our knee-jerk reaction to that old belief yet. It still overrides our acceptance of the spacious present, or at least our conscious working relationship with said present.

Yet, as we so well know, when the spacious present becomes our platform of being, when we really make the conscious shift in our thinking that allows us to use our knowledge of the spacious present, we're home free—we're in the ultimate position to create our realities with conscious understanding. And that, according to Seth, is his main message to the world, and the next step in the evolution of our consciousness.

And that is also why, as I mentioned earlier, I chose to write this book from the "top" down, rather than the "bottom" up—from All That Is to action, to identity, to consciousness, to physical reality; and a discussion of the process of creation, which is identical for all consciousness, no matter whether it is "in" physical reality or is a grand psychic gestalt that creates worlds. That is, I didn't start with the physical self, awash in its beliefs in a concrete physical world honed through cause and effect, and try to talk my way out of it. I chose, instead, to start by virtually ignoring the physical world, except as effects caused by consciousness in the spacious present.

Why? Because it's the true, the one-and-only, picture. *Everything else is camouflage*, so why on earth waste our time by dismantling illusion in a quest to find truth? Why not skip to the truth and determine, instead, how it creates illusion? That's the ultimate quest, the freeing quest; in my opinion, the only quest worth its salt in maximum knowledge.

But, it's always more than just about the quest, isn't it? Why quest unless there's a practical reason, a comfortable outcome that has meaning to us in our physical reality existence? So, a quest of the sort Seth suggests can end up as our practical ticket out of debilitating experiences, and into a more steady stream of refreshing outcomes. So questing isn't the answer, it's the path. And what's the million dollar magical ingredient that pushes us from questing into change so great it results in those refreshing outcomes consistently? There's only one answer that fits the criteria, and it is trust.

Trust starts with knowledge, or the definition of the framework we are within, and continues with integration. Knowledge, by itself, does not lead to trust. And full integration does not work until we are so comfortable with an alternate way of thinking it becomes natural. And as long as we hold such a strong inner acceptance of linear time, we cannot effectively use our knowledge of ourselves as action, and all it implies, to reach a place of absolute trust. And that is our challenge, or as Seth calls it, our learning process. And that challenge to our thinking about who we are, and what we're capable of, will eventually lead us to, as Seth says, a land of psyche and reality that represents unimpeded nature. Or, as I think of it, living a safe universe.

The Ultimate Definition of Self

As you so well know, this book is all about living a safe universe by redefining the self. And to what purpose? So we can trust. Because that's where the quest ends. It can start with trusting All That Is, but in some way that's a remote kind of trust, removed from us and our daily interactive events. It can continue with trusting our inner self, and maybe our entity, but that's also a remote kind of trust, because like trusting All That Is, it's not called into moment-by-moment use throughout our days. And the same goes for trusting a safe universe and the flow of creation. Unless we bring trust closer to home, it stays a quest, not an outcome.

The final leap of faith that takes us from questing to results has to be the trusting of our self, an intimate, always constant trusting. As Seth tells us in many different ways, we are miracles of creation and creators of miracles. We are All That Is expressing itself as identity which is conscious of itself, using action to create realities. Because we are part of All That Is, we share its ability not only to create, but to be within our creations. Or, better said, our *inability* to be apart from our creations.

And if we cannot be apart, then we must understand and trust the package of divine gifts that define us. Since we cannot be separated from All That Is, we are integral to its three dilemmas of creation. We come from identity and action and consciousness, and we use the spacious present, significances, suggestion, the moment point, probabilities, and our mental acts as our playing field of creation.

But we not only use this playing field, we *are* the playing field, because the playing field is part of All That Is. We *are* our spacious present, our significances, our suggestions, our moment points, our probabilities and our mental acts. We *are* our own reality, never found anywhere but within our own identity. And, of course, we are our inner self and entity, we are the guiding force of our self, as well as being our self.

This, then, is the *ultimate* redefinition of the self. This is who we are and why we can create. We *are* creation, not simply the created. When we forget we are creation, we become so entwined in the created part of our self we stop trusting. Trust must come from remembering—and living—the truth of our self, moment by moment. It cannot stay remote and make any sustainable difference in our life.

Seth says we stand within the miracle of ourselves and ask for signs. It's our time to stop asking for signs and live our miracle. It's time to trust our amazing selves. Seth says it can be effortless. Let us believe him and make it so. Let us seriously, and with enthusiasm, explore the unofficial thresholds where we begin, and which define us and our creative abilities.

My sincere best wishes, my friends,

Lynda

Notes

Introduction

    1. Jane Roberts, *The "Unknown" Reality, Vol. One*, Session 687

Chapter 1: Starting Our Search for Trust

    1. Jane Roberts, *The "Unknown" Reality, Vol. Two*, Session 728

    2. Jane Roberts, *Seth Speaks*, Session 551

  3-4. Sue Watkins, *Conversations With Seth, Vol. Two*, Chapter 12

    5. Jane Roberts, *The Personal Sessions, Book 3*, 10/20/75

    6. Jane Roberts, *The Nature of Personal Reality*, Session 663

    7. Jane Roberts, *The "Unknown" Reality, Vol. One*, Session 687

    8. Jane Roberts, *The Magical Approach*, Session 14

    9. Jane Roberts, *The Personal Sessions, Book 3*, Session 758

Chapter 2: All That Is

    1. Jane Roberts, *Dreams, "Evolution," and Value Fulfillment, Vol. 1*, Session 882

  2-7. Jane Roberts, *The Early Sessions, Book 3*, Session 138

Chapter 3: The Spacious Present

    1. Sue Watkins, *Conversations With Seth, Vol. Two*, Chapter 12

    2. Jane Roberts, *The Early Sessions, Book 9*, Session 425

    3. Jane Roberts, *The Early Sessions, Book 2*, Session 51

  4-5. Jane Roberts, *The Early Sessions, Book 1*, Session 41

    6. Jane Roberts, *The Early Sessions, Book 6*, Session 249

  7-9. Jane Roberts, *The Seth Material*, Chapter 10

  10. Jane Roberts, *The Early Sessions, Book 1*, Session 41

  11. Jane Roberts, *The Early Sessions, Book 3*, Session 133

12. Jane Roberts, *Dreams, "Evolution," and Value Fulfillment, Vol. 1*, Session 884

Chapter 4: Significances

1. Jane Roberts, *The Nature of the Psyche*, Session 788
2. Jane Roberts, *The Early Sessions, Book 1*, Session 41

Chapter 5: Suggestion/Mental Acts

1. Jane Roberts, *The Early Sessions, Book 4*, Session 163
2. Jane Roberts, *The Seth Material*, Chapter 10
3. Jane Roberts, *Seth Speaks*, Session 568
4. Jane Roberts, *The Individual and the Nature of Mass Events*, Session 830
5. Jane Roberts, *The Nature of Personal Reality*, Session 625
6. Jane Roberts, *Seth Speaks*, Appendix, ESP Class Session, January 12, 1971
7-10. Jane Roberts, *The Early Sessions, Book 4*, Session 163
11. Jane Roberts, *The Individual and the Nature of Mass Events*, Session 830

Chapter 6: The Moment Point/Present

1. Jane Roberts, *Seth Speaks,* Session 514.
2. Jane Roberts, *The Nature of Personal Reality*, Session 654.
3. Jane Roberts, *The "Unknown" Reality, Vol. One,* Session 681
4. Jane Roberts, *The "Unknown" Reality, Vol. One*, Session 684

Chapter 7: Probabilities

1. Jane Roberts, *Seth Speaks*, Session 514
2-3. Jane Roberts, *The Early Sessions, Book 5*, Session 234
4-6. Jane Roberts, *The Early Sessions, Book 9*, Session 438
7. Jane Roberts, *Seth Speaks*, Chapter 16
8. Jane Roberts, *The Early Sessions, Book 9*, Session 438

9. Jane Roberts, *The Seth Material*, Chapter 9

10. Jane Roberts, *Seth Speaks*, Session 566

11. Jane Roberts, *The Nature of Personal Reality*, Session 656

Chapter 8: The Entity and Inner Self

1. Jane Roberts, *Seth, Dreams and Projections of Consciousness*, Excerpts from Session 23

2. Jane Roberts, *Seth Speaks*, Session 512

3. Jane Roberts, *The Seth Material*, Session 509

4. Jane Roberts, *The Early Sessions, Book 4*, Session 178

5. Jane Roberts, *The Early Sessions, Book 7*, Session 308

6. Jane Roberts, *The Early Sessions, Book 4*, Session 163

7. Jane Roberts, *The Early Sessions, Book 2*, Session 70

Chapter 9: Trust

1. Jane Roberts, *The Individual and the Nature of Mass Events*, Session 826

2. Jane Roberts, *The Seth Material*, Chapter 18

3. Jane Roberts, *The Afterdeath Journal of an American Philosopher*, Chapter 13

4. Jane Roberts, *The "Unknown" Reality, Vol. Two*, Session 733

5   Jane Roberts, *The Individual and the Nature of Mass Events*, Session 872

6. Jane Roberts, *Seth Speaks*, Session 550

7. Jane Roberts, *The Personal Sessions, Book 3*, Session 11/3/75

8. Jane Roberts, *The Nature of Personal Reality*, Session 677

Chapter 11: Learning to Trust the Moment Point

1. Jane Roberts, *The Early Sessions, Book 5*, Session 226

2. Jane Roberts, *Seth Speaks*, Session 575

3. Jane Roberts, *The Nature of Personal Reality*, Session 658

4. Jane Roberts, Deleted Session

5. Jane Roberts, *The Early Sessions, Book 5*, Session 220

6. Jane Roberts, Deleted Session
7. Jane Roberts, *The Magical Approach*, Session 14
8. Jane Roberts, Deleted Session, 8-14-78
9. Jane Roberts, *The Way Toward Health*, Chapter 4
10. Jane Roberts, *The Nature of the Psyche*, Session 787
11. Jane Roberts, *Dreams, "Evolution," and Value Fulfillment, Vol. 1*, Introductory Essays, Essay 7
12. Jane Roberts, *The Nature of Personal Reality*, Session 616
13. Jane Roberts, *The Nature of Personal Reality*, Session 654
14. Jane Roberts, *The God of Jane*, Chapter 2, Session for Oct. 24, 1977
15. Jane Roberts, *The Nature of Personal Reality*, Session 644
16. Sue Watkins, *Conversations With Seth, Vol. 2*, Chapter 13
17. Jane Roberts, *The Nature of Personal Reality*, Session 656
18. Jane Roberts, *The Magical Approach*, Session 12
19. Sue Watkins, *Conversations With Seth, Vol. 2*, Chapter 20

Chapter 12: Living With Conscious Understanding

1. Jane Roberts, *The Individual and the Nature of Mass Events*, Session 834
2. Jane Roberts, *The Personal Sessions, Book 3*, 10/20/75
3. Jane Roberts, *The "Unknown" Reality, Vol. Two*, Introductory Notes by Robert F. Butts

Seth/Jane Roberts Books

Books by Jane Roberts, Dictated by Seth

Seth Speaks: The Eternal Validity of the Soul
The Nature of Personal Reality: A Seth Book
The "Unknown" Reality: A Seth Book, Volumes One& Two
The Nature of the Psyche: Its Human Expression
The Individual and the Nature of Mass Events
Dreams, "Evolution," and Value Fulfillment, Volumes One & Two
The Magical Approach: Seth Speaks About the Art of Creative Living
The Way Toward Health

Books by Jane Roberts, Related to Her Work with Seth

How to Develop Your ESP Power
The Seth Material
Adventures in Consciousness: An Introduction to Aspect Psychology
Dialogues of the Soul and Mortal Self in Time
Psychic Politics: An Aspect Psychology Book
The World View of Paul Cezanne
The Afterdeath Journal of an American Philosopher: The World View of
    William James
Emir's Education in the Proper Use of Magical Powers
The God of Jane: A Psychic Manifesto
If We Live Again: Or, Public Magic and Private Love
Seth, Dreams and Projections of Consciousness
The Oversoul Seven Trilogy: The Education of Oversoul Seven; The
    Further Education of Oversoul Seven; Oversoul Seven and the
    Museum of Time

Books Comprised of Sessions not in Original Books

The Early Sessions, Vol. 1-9; The Personal Sessions, Vol. 1-7; The Early
Class Sessions, Vol. 1-4

Lynda Madden Dahl, award-winning author of five Seth-based books, coined the term conscious creation with her first book, *Beyond the Winning Streak: Using Conscious Creation to Consistently Win at Life*. Her whole focus since reading her first Seth book in 1984 has been to understand the nature of reality and integrate that knowledge into a working order in her thoughts and, by extension, life.

Lynda is co-founder of Seth Network International, the global meeting place for Seth readers. She published a quarterly magazine, *Reality Change: The Global Seth Journal*, for seven years, and has produced numerous Seth conferences and been a speaker at many others.

SETH NETWORK
INTERNATIONAL

Co-founded by Lynda Dahl as the
global meeting place for Seth readers

....

www.sethnet.org   contactus@sethnet.org

....

FACEBOOK

Become friends with Lynda and many other Seth
readers on Facebook at Lynda Madden Dahl

....

Also on **FACEBOOK**,
please check out the following pages:
**

Seth/Jane Roberts Books and Info
Seth Network International
Beyond the Winning Streak – by Lynda Madden Dahl
Ten Thousand Whispers – by Lynda Madden Dahl
The Wizards of Consciousness – by Lynda Madden Dahl
The Book of Fallacies – by Lynda Madden Dahl
Living a Safe Universe – by Lynda Madden Dahl
Bridging Science and Spirit – by Norman Friedman
The Hidden Domain – by Norman Friedman

Made in the USA
Lexington, KY
15 January 2013